Learning French?
How to Make it Happen

THE MORE RECENT BOOKS
OF *LEARN FRENCH AT HOME*

—*12 Short suspense Stories in French for French Learners*: *Le bruit des vagues* (**Nr. 1, 2017**); *Le pays de l'amour* (**Nr. 2, 2018**); *Le trésor* (**Nr. 3, 2019**); *Le chat qui parle* (**Nr. 4, 2020**). Glossaries, grammar tips, cultural notes, exercises with solutions and full audio for each story. Paperback and eBooks (pdf) with audio links.

—*French Grammar and Beyond.* Easy explanations in English of French grammar, with 200 exercises and solutions. For beginners to intermediate levels. Paperback and eBook (pdf). 2020.

—*Traveling in France: Essential Communication for the Smart Tourist.* Easy guide of everyday French expressions and vocabulary indispensable for foreigners traveling in France. Paperback and eBook (pdf) with audio links. New edition 2020.

—*Learn French with Fun Activities.* **A Workbook for kids and teenagers, with songs, poems, exercises (with solutions) and games.** For parents or French teachers who can guide the children through the suggested means of studying. Paperback and eBook (pdf) with audio links. New edition 2020.

—*English-French Glossary of the United Nations, NGOs and International Relations.* 12,000 Words and Expressions About the New Challenges of Today's World. Paperback and eBook (pdf). 2020.

www.learnfrenchathome.com/french-audio-books

All these books are also available on Amazon:
amazon.com/author/annickstevenson

Our Magazine

French Accent Magazine: The unique and **FREE** e-magazine for French learners, with a central theme and articles on politics, culture, grammar, etc.. Scenarios and vocabulary with audio links are included as well.

www.learnfrenchathome.com/french-accent-magazine

Learning French?
How to Make it Happen

A Self-Help Guide
With a Multitude of Tips
and Tricks

Annick Stevenson

A publication of Learn French at Home

Author: Annick Stevenson

Published by: *Learn French at Home*
Website: www.learnfrenchathome.com
Date of Publication: 2020
ISBN: 9798663749411

This book is published in three versions: paperback, Kindle and eBook. With the purchase of the paperback or Kindle versions, a free copy of the eBook will be available. The eBook version is in pdf format. See page 130 how to access to your free copy of the eBook version.

Cover: Portraits of the students of Learn French at Home who wrote testimonies for this book. From left to right:
—top: Hrant Yardumian, Ann Bingley Gallops and Michael Storrings (© Philippe Matsas).
—bottom: Laverne Fryxell, Steven Sorenson and Patricia Pattison.
© DR

Back cover: Annick Stevenson
© DR

... ce qui frappait mes yeux dans les rues,
dans les cafés [...], un film
bouleversant, une joyeuse conversation
amicale, une belle page de roman :
tout cela pouvait irriguer et fertiliser
la langue qui me traversait désormais...

"Une langue venue d'ailleurs"

(...what was striking for my eyes in the streets,
in the cafés [...], a moving film, a joyful, friendly,
conversation, a beautiful page from a novel:
all this could irrigate and fertilize
the language that now ran through me.)

Akira Mizubayashi,
Japanese writer and university teacher
of French in Tokyo, writes all his books
in French and is quite well known in France

CONTENTS

Foreword   Page 13

1. **The appeal of learning French**   Page 17

2. **Motivation and determination
   are keys to success**   Page 23

   Michael: "*On trips to Paris, I have taken
   painting classes taught in French*"   Page 27

3. **Don't be afraid!**   Page 29

4. **The importance of having a good teacher**   Page 35

   Laverne: "*I associate with small groups
   of French learners*"   Page 43

5. **The right balance between discipline
   and pleasure**   Page 47

6. **Listen to your teacher, to a song,**
   watch a movie...   Page 51

   Steven: *"I prefer old, classic French movies"*   Page 55

7. **Speak French with the French!**
   They will love it   Page 59

8. **A few tips on how to address French people**   Page 65

   Ann: *"I enjoy reading mystery novels*
   that feature a lot of dialogue"   Page 71

9. **Get in the habit of reading, anything**   Page 75

10. **Write in French, you'll make it**
    with some help   Page 79

    Hrant: *"I acquired the 'habit' of making*
    French friends"   Page 85

11. **Yes, you'll have a few hurdles to overcome:**
    Our tips to deal with them   Page 87

12. **Discouraged? It happens,**
    and it's no big deal   Page 95

    Patti: *"I learn a lot by reading novels in French"*   Page 99

13. **Practice: Essential if you want**
    to make it happen   Page 101

14. The fun part: Using French expressions, and realizing how being fluent has changed you   Page 107

Jim, our model student   Page 113

15. Children love learning French, too!   Page 117

ANNEX: Our suggestions of useful resources   Page 123

FOREWORD

TAKING PAINTING CLASSES in French when he's in Paris is one of the ways an American artist living in New York, Michael, has chosen to get to speak and hear French, a language he's passionate about. Devising their own methods to remember French words or expressions, reading French books, watching movies, taking every opportunity to make French friends... These are a just few ways that the students who appear on the cover of this book have found to improve their knowledge of French in parallel with their regular lessons with teachers of Learn French at Home, the first ever French school on Skype.

The main purpose of *Learning French? How to Make it Happen* is to make it very clear to those of you who want to learn French that you can succeed, and how to get there. This book will give you all the advice and a multitude of tips, tricks and tools to help you along the way of your learning journey.

When Céline Van Loan and Vincent Anthonioz created in 2004 this innovative way of teaching French, it was to respond to a need that was obvious to so many people all over the world. Since then, Learn French at Home has helped more than 3,000 students of various ages, origins and backgrounds. Since the beginning of the confinement in early 2020, taking private French lessons via Skype or Zoom has become for many a necessity. The demand exploded.

Regular lessons with a teacher, face-to-face or rather screen-to-screen, have proven to be the best way to seriously learn a language, as so many students tell us everyday. However, as good as the lessons are, it's highly recommended to supplement them with a variety of enjoyable activities to do on your own.

The testimonies that some of our outstanding students wrote for this book are the best confirmation that if you follow the same type of path, you'll undoubtedly reach your learning objectives.

We also remind you all throughout this book that you shouldn't, in any case, feel intimidated or afraid and that you will progress even if you go through phases of discouragement. Getting the right balance between discipline and pleasure is also a very important part of the learning process. Having fun learning with a nice, friendly and encouraging teacher and through various motivating activities, helps you considerably to gain confidence, which is the only way to progress and to fully enjoy the voyage.

I hope this motivational book will help you feel more at home with the French language, to appreciate the progress you make and to take pleasure in it!

Annick Stevenson

Note that throughout the book, instead of "him/her," we have used the pronoun "they," according to the current usage.

1. THE APPEAL OF LEARNING FRENCH

THE SPREAD OF THE CORONAVIRUS all over the world, country by country, was for many the trigger for learning a new language. Many people from all walks of life who found themselves confined at home chose French as their new language or decided it was the perfect time to enhance their knowledge. It was the consecration of something they had been thinking about for a long time but were not ready or motivated enough to take the plunge.

The appeal of learning French isn't new, though. When Céline and Vincent created Learn French at home, it was already to address a real need at the time, as explained in the foreword.

There are so many reasons why people want to learn French. Here are a few of them from our students:
—to work for a French-speaking company or an international company with agencies or branches in France;
—to get ready for long missions in French-speaking Africa if you work for the United Nations or an NGO;
—to work for an international organization;
—to prepare for a press conference or briefing in French in France or Africa;
—to prepare for various types of exams;
—to complete traditional school studies, which is the case for most of the children we are teaching (an important part of our activity);
—to move to a French-speaking country;
—to get ready for a trip to France, etc.

Learning French for the love of France and the language

However, three quarters of the 3,000 students we've been teaching since 2004, of every age and background, are learning French simply because they love France and the language. They want to be able to understand a French movie, communicate with French people, discover more about French history and culture, etc.

The French language seems to have become very trendy recently in Anglophone countries, especially in the United States, maybe more so than a few years ago. When we ask our students to be more specific about the reasons that motivated them to learn French, they first reply that they want to study the language because France is a country with a rich history and culture. They love the art, beauty and diversity of the countryside, of the cities and of their architecture and everything else that makes France famous. They're particularly attracted by the spirit of independence, luxury products, cheese, museums, wines, freedom of speech, gastronomy, literature, French cinema, castles in the Loire region, French cartoons, croissants, not to forget romantic love...

These reasons reflect the very goals that each student sets while starting to learn the language. Some of them have a deadline, some not. Which means that the appeal of learning French can remain very strong for months or years, as long as the goals haven't been reached.

Don't be intimidated! French is a rather recent language

Some of our new students tell us that they are quite intimidated in learning the language of Molière, Voltaire and Rousseau that they consider to be very classy and academic. They even sometimes see it as a very tall and fearsome mountain to climb!

No, the French language is not an unattainable peak to ascend but a series of small, charming, green and lovely hills that are constantly evolving. In reality, the French language as we know it today is mainly the result of the chaos that preceded and followed the French Revolution that started in 1789 and brought to Paris freedom fighters from all the regions — each of them having its own dialect or *patois*, which severely complicated communication between them. It was mainly to help revolutionaries understand each other that a unified French language was created. As such, it can be considered a "democratic" language and not at all an "academic language" as some intellectuals pretend. Before the Revolution, 75% of French citizens did not speak French! My own grandmother, who was from the Provence region and who spoke *provençal*, never learned to speak French.

Parlez-vous franglais ?

Over the years, this language born during the Revolution has been influenced by many others: North African, German, the Scandinavian languages, Italian, Spanish, Dutch, Japanese...

But today, it's undoubtedly the English language that has infiltrated the most profoundly the French language. In spite of some criticisms among French intellectuals, the Anglo-Saxon wave seems impossible to stop. Especially in French or international companies there are more and more English expressions creeping into the language.

Our students always say that it comes as a nice surprise to find so many English words while speaking with French people or reading articles, blogs or posts on social networks. And they often find it very amusing to see how they are used and transformed.

Therefore, when they want to express something, for example to a salesperson or a waiter in a bistro or restaurant and they don't know the right French word, they are tempted to say it in English. Sometimes it works. Not always, though!

Learning French strengthens the brain

It has been proven from many sources that learning a new language improves your knowledge, your understanding, your expertise, your awareness and, therefore, makes you a more attractive and engaging person. But it has many other crucial benefits. Learning French, or any new language, is also well known to be really excellent to improve one's memory, the capacity of one's brain and even to reduce the risk of dementia or Alzheimer's disease.

Several students well over 70 or 80 years old have told us that they were very happy to discover that studying French helped improve their memory and mental capacities. They said it was like a fountain of youth!

The pleasure of learning more about French culture

One of the magic aspects of learning a new language is that you have the chance to discover a totally new culture. The more you study it, the more you feel the need to immerse yourself in that culture and to increase your knowledge of it. You will see that this, too, has positive effects on your mental capacities.

Learning about all the cultural differences, as you'll discover over time, is really fascinating and makes French lessons much more interesting and fun. During the Skype or Zoom discussions that all our teachers have with their students, the specificities of French culture are constantly evoked, discussed and explained. They are very often the opportunity for a good laugh!

You'll see that when you've reached a more advanced level, you'll invariably be motivated to know even more...

TO REMEMBER FROM CHAPTER 1

• **Three quarters of our students learn French simply because they love France and the language.** They tell us what appeals to them in France.

• **Don't be intimidated by the so-called "academic" language.** The French language is actually quite recent. It was born with the French Revolution as a more "democratic language" that everyone could share. **Before the Revolution, 75% of French citizens did not speak French!**

• **The French language is constantly evolving.** The last decade has seen a real **invasion of English terms and expressions.**

• **When you don't know the French word** when explaining something to a salesperson or a waiter in a restaurant in France, **try the English one!** I doesn't always work, though.

• Learning French is excellent to **improve one's memory, one's mental capacities and even to reduce the risk of dementia and Alzheimer's disease.** Some students say it is like a fountain of youth!

• While studying the French language you **discover many fascinating aspects of French culture.**

2. MOTIVATION AND DETERMINATION ARE KEYS TO SUCCESS

MOTIVATION IS OBVIOUSLY one of the main criteria when we learn a language. It is the driving force of all the efforts all French learners make and, as long as they haven't reached their goal, the motivation will remain as strong as it was at the beginning.

We can say the same of all our students. During the first interview by Skype or Zoom, we try not only to assess their level and their specific objectives but to understand their degree of motivation. When a person tells us: "I would like to try but I am not sure if I can make it, if I will be able to learn a new language, I don't really need to speak French so it is not very important for me," etc., we know that it will certainly be more difficult than for someone who is highly motivated. Fortunately most of them are, which helps considerably in the success.

Desire, a major element

First and foremost, there has to be the desire. Without desire, often associated with curiosity, another important element that will enhance your will to succeed, there is no motivation. And motivation is something that has to come from yourself. It will help you maintain the will to learn and also to feel the pleasure each time you notice you've made some progress. Your French teacher can only encourage you, stimulate your desire and motivation by helping you overcome your fear, hesitation, lack of confidence and increase your knowledge, patiently, at your speed and according to your level and wishes. But your teacher cannot create your own motivation and your desire on your behalf.

Once you're sufficiently motivated, what is needed is determination, as is the case for any discipline. Desire is what keeps the flame of motivation alive, but it's determination and commitment to an unrelenting pursuit of your objective that will enable you to make your way along the path of learning you have embarked on, until you've reached your goal.

How to sustain your determination?

No matter how obvious these sayings are, it is so easy after a few weeks, months or years, while you are busy with many tasks, professional or family constraints, tight schedules or hampered by psychological obstacles, to ease up on your concentration and determination. Moreover, even if you really want to reach your objectives, it is very natural to be, from time to time, overcome by tiredness, loss of attention or simply laziness that may prevent you from making the necessary effort and keeping a regular schedule of study.

To reach your objectives and to keep your determination, here are a few recommendations:

—Follow a reasonable pace of study. For example, take a French lesson once a week instead of committing yourself to several times a week, a pace that you may not be able to follow.

—Keep your objectives constantly in mind. Try not to be distracted by other undertakings.

—Be disciplined.

—Establish a few habits: following a regular schedule of lessons, browsing through some information in French on the web, listening to French podcasts at a regular pace, etc. And stick to them.

—Be confident, trust yourself. You know you can make it.

—Be patient. Don't believe in anyone who tells you that you can be fluent in three months! It just won't happen.

—Visualize your results. Imagine yourself succeeding at your job appointment or exam, being able to communicate more easily in French during your next stay in Paris, watching a French movie and understanding it, etc.

—Seek support from French friends or acquaintances, participate to French events organized by groups of Francophiles, join French groups on social media...

—Have fun, enjoy the journey! If you're really motivated, the pleasure starts on the very first day of your new commitment, and it will never cease all along your road to success.

—Adjust your plan and pace of study each time you realize a change is needed. It is crucial to adapt it to any change that may occur in your life or to your availability and possibilities. Remain realistic!

TO REMEMBER FROM CHAPTER 2

- **Motivation is a principal driving force when learning a new language.**

- **Without desire**, often associated with **curiosity, there is no motivation.**

- **Motivation is something that you have to feel by yourself.** Your French teacher can only encourage you, stimulate your desire and motivation by helping you overcome your fear, hesitation and lack of confidence.

- **Another essential ingredient for achievement is determination.** Read our advice on how to sustain your determination.

© Philippe Matsas

Michael: "On trips to Paris, I have taken painting classes taught in French"

ONE OF THE DIFFICULTIES of learning French for me is not being able to speak it everyday or to be fully immersed in French speaking environment. That is why I eagerly search out ways to get to speak and hear French.

On some of my trips to Paris, I have taken painting classes that were taught in French. In my city of New York, I try to go to events where French is spoken — like book readings. I also watch French TV at least one hour per day.

I love listening to French podcasts and download French novels on my kindle. If there are words that I don't know, I can click on the word and the definition comes up immediately!

I dedicate French time into my schedule. I think the most important thing to do is homework and it may be obvious but sometimes it is really hard to find the time to do it. I also try doing French word searches or crosswords.

"Don't worry if you make mistakes, you don't need to be perfect"

Further, one important thing that I tell myself when I am in a French-speaking country is to speak. Don't worry if you make mistakes, you don't need to be perfect.

Michael Storrings
Artist
New York City
www.storrings.com

A beautiful demonstration of Michael's love for Paris!

Michael has been a student at Learn French at Home since 2017. He loves Paris and the French way of life. Even though he is a very busy artist, he's always made time to work on his French. He dives right into the language whenever he can; he is passionate about the language and truly enjoys a good conversation in French.

3. DON'T BE AFRAID!

BREAKING THE FEAR BARRIER that you inevitably encounter when you learn a new language is fundamental if you want to progress. We cannot stress this very important aspect too much. Be brave, courageous, open and don't be shy if you do not feel comfortable speaking French in the very beginning, and you will soon notice that the pressure this fear is exerting on you will lessen. Breaking the fear barrier, and doing it repeatedly each time you feel afraid again, is a necessary step when learning a new language

Our experience has taught us that our students who study French with passion or personal motivation are more successful than those who are hampered or restricted by the fear of not being able to succeed. As we explained earlier, the French language is not a high mountain to climb but a language that constantly changes and in which more and more foreign words, especially those from English, are integrated, which makes it easier for English-speaking learners. This is yet another good reason not to be afraid!

Avoid seeking too much advice

Nobody but you can have a complete understanding of why you have decided to study French, of your objectives and personal interests. Nobody should be able to discourage you from following the learning path that you have mapped out for yourself. Therefore, we suggest that you avoid seeking advice, comments or recommendations, unless it is from someone who fully understands what you are doing and who shares the same enthusiasm for the French language. It's better to ask someone you trust and who can really help you, such as a member of the network of friends and French people that you have established, as we proposed in the previous chapter. By doing so, by just continuing your study at a comfortable pace, you don't have any reason not to be totally self-confident or to fear the judgment of anyone else. As much as you can, try to remain cool, and feel as secure as you can.

Don't be ashamed to talk

Another type of fear is that of feeling ashamed to speak broken French to people you don't know. This is another barrier you will have to break in your learning process and you will feel much better when you have succeeded. The only solution is not to hesitate to speak in French any time you may have the opportunity, without worrying about what others will think. You don't need to be perfect, as Michael said on page 28.

The best way to get used to speaking in public is to have regular face-to-face (Skype-to-Skype or Zoom-to-Zoom) conversations with a French teacher. Many of our students told us how afraid they were when they started their French lessons. But most of the time, after just a few lessons the fear has vanished and they feel upbeat and positive about talking to French people.

Your teacher is not the only person who will be patient with you when you try speaking French with them. You will see that the French persons with whom you make this effort will respond positively and be ready to help you.

We will revisit in depth later in the book the importance of speaking and of not being shy about doing so.

Accept the idea that you will make mistakes

Absolutely every individual who goes through the process of learning, in whatever field or art, knows exactly what it is to make mistakes and has to accept it, deal with it and learn from it. Almost every student has had the experience of feeling stupid after having said something awkward or inappropriate. We know very well that feeling, too. Your French native instructor had to learn English, and sometimes other languages, to become a teacher. We all remember making mistakes of which we were ashamed at the moment, before starting laughing about it. Relating our own blunders is often a very good way to break the ice or to lighten the atmosphere at a dinner party!

At the end of one of our immersion workshops in California, when students and teachers had the last dinner together in a nice Italian restaurant, a student shared with us the following anecdote: "Once in an hotel in France, I wanted to have a drink. I saw a glass dispenser in a corner where hotel guests could help themselves. One couldn't see what was inside because of the amber glassware. In front of it there was a little note on which it was written *Vide*." This means "empty" in French but our student didn't know that. She tried to help herself by opening the spigot but couldn't get anything. She described to us the face that the receptionist made when she asked him, with insistence, that she would like to have some "*vide*" but didn't know how to help herself! We all laughed and started describing similar funny adventures.

So, don't be afraid to make mistakes and to have the feeling of looking stupid from time to time. And you will see later in the book that more and more French people make a lot of mistakes in their own language, too...!

Don't be too hard on yourself

This is another important recommendation that we can give you. Some students are too hard on themselves when they have the feeling that they are not making as much progress as they would like. Most of the time this feeling does not correspond to reality. Even if you think that you are not progressing, this is not always the case. You never stop learning, memorizing, enriching your vocabulary. And do not forget that learning a language is a personal commitment. It is very similar to yoga in this respect, also given the fact that your own pace is very personal. You should never, ever, try to compare your progress to that made by other students. More importantly, make the best of it and enjoy the process!

TO REMEMBER FROM CHAPTER 3

• **Breaking the fear barrier** that you inevitably encounter when you learn a new language is **fundamental**.

• **Be brave, courageous, open, and don't be shy** if you do not feel comfortable speaking French in the very beginning, and you will soon notice that the pressure this fear is exerting on you will lessen.

• **Avoid** seeking too much advice.

• **Don't be ashamed to talk.**

• **Accept the idea that, like everybody, you will make mistakes — and learn to laugh about them!**

• **Don't be too hard on yourself.**

4. THE IMPORTANCE OF HAVING A GOOD TEACHER

THERE IS A MULTITUDE of very well-done websites or apps from which you can learn some French, listen to French pronunciation, do auto-corrected and fun exercises on every aspect of the grammar and test and improve your vocabulary. Most of them are excellent tools and we strongly recommend that you take advantage of them, not only at the beginning but also later on as a very useful complement to your study. They provide important follow-up practice, they enable you to consolidate what you have learned and to obtain further explanations, to get the right meaning of certain words or expressions and to translate them, to reassure you that you have made good progress or simply to have fun while playing word games. We always advise our students to use the best ones as often as possible, as the more you work and practice, the more you progress.

However, learning alone through any app or webpage device isn't enough. You will never be able to become fluent if you have no teacher gently correcting your pronunciation and explaining how to express what you want to say in French so that you can be understood by French people or write without making too many errors. You need to have someone who can accompany you during this fascinating journey of learning a language, someone who will be your guide while you are progressing towards your personal objectives.

Someone who can explain to you the nuances of the French language and provide you with some essential insights into the culture, who will give you specific and appropriate homework and escort you at each step along the way. But when we say that a teacher is indispensable, we mean a "good" teacher.

What is a good teacher?

There are many definitions of a "good" or of the "best teacher." From our experience, a good teacher is someone who, at first, is willing to get to know you, to listen to you, who pays a lot of attention to you and who is truly interested in who you are, what you like, what you intend or hope to do, someone who cares about you. Second, a good teacher is someone who is able to adapts their way of teaching to your style, your personality, your interests, your wishes and makes sure to help you in the best way possible. It is someone with whom you have, beginning with the first lesson, explained your objectives — who may even have helped you to set them if you have felt unsecure or uncertain — and who does their best to help you achieve them.

A good teacher sees you as a unique person, has consideration and respect for you, does not, under any circumstance, judge or criticize you, understands you, is positive, is able to reassure you, gives you intelligent and useful feedback and does not allow you to get discouraged. With such an instructor, you'll always feel comfortable, be able to share your thoughts and even have fun and thoroughly enjoy each lesson. A good teacher is not only someone who teaches something and builds on your abilities, but also someone who encourages you to think and question.

What kind of learner are you?

Figuring out how you learn is an important aspect of successful language learning. If the teacher teaches in a way that does not suit your style of learning, you might lose interest in the lesson and give up the idea of learning French, which would be a real shame. Many students are not quite sure what stimulates them until they have started their French learning experience. Perhaps you enjoy best studying through games? Or you prefer trying to express yourself through casual conversations? Or perhaps you need to get a lot of feedback in order to gain confidence in speaking? Perhaps you need to write everything down in order to be able to memorize the new information? Some people enjoy the challenge of understanding the fine points of grammar while others are put off by it. Certain students work best through repetition and others need many visual aids.

The best way to find out your style of learning is by taking private lessons. A teacher who gets to know you very well after some time should be able to understand what stimulates you, your pace of learning and which method works best for you. If not, then do not hesitate to tell the teacher what appeals to you the most. Being able to personalize the lessons to your objectives, motivations and pace of learning is what makes a good teacher. The lesson experience should feel comfortable and at the same time stimulating.

Beware of teaching that is too "academic"

This is the reason why we do not consider that teaching French, or any other language, should be done in a too academic way. Instead, it should be done in a very personalized and positive way, so that the student gets the maximum out of their lessons and makes real progress. There are many schools for adults all over the world with teachers who are able to teach in this way. Unfortunately, there are also many French instructors who have been influenced by the rather rigid French education system: following a pre-formatted program or book, without too much personalization or feedback, and sometimes not much encouragement — if any at all. Not all French teachers in the academic system (either in France or French studies programs all over the world) are so strict, far from it. This does   unfortunately happen and you will rapidly be aware of it.

One of the major problems with academic teaching is that you may not learn common everyday French, the "real" French that French people speak. We would advise you not to pay too much attention to pretentious and glossy advertisements from schools with a reputation that may not always be justified.

We hope that, whomever you find, they will be a "good" teacher. If not, you may wish to find someone else... This is why we offer you one more piece of advice: Do not commit yourself for too many lessons or for a full program before first having had the experience of a few lessons, i.e. before knowing your teacher better and being sure that you feel completely comfortable with them.

Learn French at Home, from a social distance

It is now time to introduce to you our language school, how it works, our experience with teaching with distance learning technology while you are comfy at home. When Céline Van Loan and Vincent Anthonioz started Learn French at Home in 2004, there were not yet any schools offering personalized one-on-one lessons on Skype with a teacher who is sincerely interested in you and who follows your progress over time. The need for such distance schooling was obvious, especially for busy professionals or students who couldn't attend regular lessons in a school. Learn French at Home could meet their needs, thanks to the use of Skype or Zoom and also to the flexibility of our teachers, all French native speakers and very good professionals who are located all over the world. Each teacher easily adapts their schedule, wherever the students live.

Before 2020, Learn French at Home was already known as a serious, caring and reputable language school. Our students appreciate the personalization and the continuous feedback during the lessons as well as the excellence, kindness and flexibility of the teachers. But when the coronavirus struck the planet, the difficulty of learning in a school or group sessions with a teacher face to face became impossible. The demand for online lessons exploded and was the confirmation that distance learning, by Skype, Zoom or other platforms, fits perfectly in today's world and is the best approach for the future. We almost doubled the number of teachers, all of them fitting perfectly to what we consider a good teacher, as we already explained: someone who is very competent but also kind, who cares, who knows how to adapt their teaching to the needs, level and pace of learning of each student, and someone who doesn't follow a rigid program but who is able to develop specific and innovative lessons for each student.

Very special students

When someone speaks about a school, they usually highlight or praise its methods, its reputation, the qualities and seriousness of its teachers and the success achieved by the students. They hardly talk of, or praise, the students themselves.

At Learn French at Home, every student is special. Not only because they come from a wide array of countries, but also due to their varied backgrounds, personalities, skills, interests and energy. We are always amazed by them. We constantly learn a lot from them, like those who gave us their testimonies for this book.

We have students who are famous artists, university teachers, writers, lawyers, adventurers, pilots, high level scientists, engineers, nurses, specialized doctors and famous surgeons, computer experts, shop owners, farmers, chefs, business owners, retired professionals or super moms, students in various fields, employees of the United Nations or humanitarian organizations working in Headquarters or in various war-torn countries, high level sportsmen, etc., and many children.

Very specialized teachers

To help all these very special students in the most effective and pro-ductive way, we are lucky to also have very special native French teachers from many different backgrounds, whose experience goes way beyond what we could expect from them in terms of the usual academic studies. Many of them speak more than three languages, have had exciting careers, hold master degrees in very different fields and all of them have lived in different countries. An explorer coming back from the Kashmir who needs to prepare TV interviews in France to talk about her book that has just been translated into French will be assigned a teacher who is a former journalist who will know what kind of questions this student may face. A United Nations official who has to prepare conferences on development in Africa will feel much more confident if their teacher has experience working for the UN and is knowledgeable about development issues. The same is true for an artist who wants to prepare for an exhibit, a scientist who has a lecture to give to a French audience, an athlete who will compete in a French-speaking country, etc.

When your teacher becomes a friend...

We have many students who started with Learn French at Home many years ago and who are still studying with us, not because they haven't succeeded in learning French but on the contrary because they always want to know more and they love their lessons! And there are others who had stopped for a while since they were too busy, who come back. Why is that? They're still very motivated and feel comfortable with their teacher, in full confidence. They all love that the lessons always take place in a relaxed and friendly atmos-phere. And what often naturally happens is that the teacher and the student become good friends. Maybe it is because you learn from home, and your teacher is also giving the lesson from their home and not from a school or an office, or because you get to know each other so well that you cannot have a lesson without chatting about personal matters... Each lesson becomes a privileged moment, such as a rendezvous with someone you are very happy to meet. There inevitably comes a time where you care for one another and feel the need to meet, just as friends usually do.

All of us, the founders of the school, as well as several teachers, have established links with some of their students which extend far beyond the French lessons. We visit each other in our respective countries, we celebrate birthdays and weddings together, etc.

TO REMEMBER FROM CHAPTER 4

• **It is essential to have a teacher**, even if you intend to work a lot on your own, or through an excellent website or app, while learning French.

• **A good teacher will be your guide** while you are progressing in your studies. Someone who can explain to you the nuances of the French language and provide you with some essential insights into the culture.

• **A good teacher sees you as a unique person**, has consideration and respect for you, does not judge or criticize you, understands you, is positive, is able to reassure you and gives you intelligent and useful feedback, and **adapts to your objectives and your way of learning**.

• **Beware of teaching that is too "academic."**

• **Learn French at Home is the perfect school for so many, and has become even more essential since learning from a distance has become the only possibility.**

• **Most of our students are very special.** See some examples.

• **Our teachers are very special, too, and specialized.**

• For many students, **their teacher, with whom they feel so comfortable, even becomes a friend** after some time...

Laverne: "I associate with small groups of French learners"

© DR

WHEN I RETIRED, I decided that I would like to learn French. I find that learning a foreign language is great to keep the brain active. It is both challenging and fun to try something different. It is even better if you had some French in your past education. Unfortunately, I did not.

First and foremost, Céline and her fellow instructors at Learn French at Home are truly caring and seasoned professionals. They are astute in identifying and customizing an individual learning experience for each student to enable them to progress in the best way.

Every teacher with whom I have worked has put me at ease and has worked with me to develop my skills. The teachers allow the students to develop both speaking and grammar skills. They allow the students to speak in French without interruption and at the same time coach them as to the proper grammar to use. Weekly homework assignments emphasize the topics discussed and those which need additional practice. Lessons are done on Skype on the computer. The student and instructor are able to exchange written comments while at the same time having face to face interaction.

"I found French literary books that were very interesting to read"

In addition, I try to spend 5-10 hours on independent French learning each week. As time allows, I use sessions on Coffee Break French. This is mainly to develop listening and interpretations skills. I also listen to podcasts online. Learn French at Home publishes a French magazine which I find very useful.

They also have a number of books and supplements which are very interesting to read, and to listen to. There is a great deal of French literature available at Amazon — books, short stories and novels.

I also watch movies in French from Amazon and Netflix. I have been viewing the TV series *Le Bazar de la Charité* and a few movies that I loved: *Les Parapluies de Cherbourg*, *Le Comte de Monte Cristo* and *Les Intouchables*. I liked *Le Fabuleux destin d'Amélie Poulain* and I also watched *Le Jeu* that I didn't like. I view all the films with French subtitles and I attempt to translate them as quickly as I can into English as I watch the films.

Whenever possible I attempt to speak French to other French speaking people in the area and I try to associate with small groups of French learners to practice speaking the language.

In addition, my husband and I try to travel to French speaking areas such as France, Montréal and Québec. I also participated in two French immersion workshops sponsored by Learn French at Home which were weekends wholly devoted to the French language. Now, I carry around my iPhone when I am away from home and I use it to check the meaning or gender of a French word as I think of it.

"Once I found a mistake in a French word, in a shoe store..."

A funny thing happened to me recently. I bought some shoes from a Canadian store in Vancouver, WA. The bag in which the store packed my shoes had French written on it.

The French phrase was: *Le Bonheur ne s'anchète pas, mais au moins vous pouvez porter des Fluevogs !* I could not recognize the French word (*s'anchète**) so I asked my French professor its meaning and I was told that the store had used incorrect French. My professor asked me to follow up with the Québec company and to inform them of their error. I was told that they already knew of the error and that I was in possession of a "unique bag." End of story.

Laverne Fryxell
Clinical Laboratory Scientist-Blood Bank Specialist (retired)
Sequim, Washington, USA

_____

*It should have been: *s'achète* (cannot be bought).

Laverne has been a student at Learn French at Home since 2017. She enjoys learning to keep her mind active. She works every week on her French. She is an exemplary student who makes sure that she always does her class homework and more. Her French verbal expression was very limited in 2017, and now Laverne can speak about most subjects. Her continuous progression has been impressive.

5. THE RIGHT BALANCE BETWEEN DISCIPLINE AND PLEASURE

AS WE SAID BEFORE, some discipline is essential when learning a language as it is with any other activity. This can take many different forms. Most of our students have established an original way to discipline themselves on a daily or weekly basis. Here are a few examples of the habits they have adopted:

—read a chapter or a few pages of a book in French once a day (with their smartphone in hand to check the unfamiliar words on their app);

—listen to audio books in French;

—subscribe to a French newspaper or magazine online and read the titles and at least one or two articles in every issue;

—participate in a Facebook, Instagram, Twitter or other social media French speaking group;

—listen regularly to some French podcasts or online videos (we give a few links in the Annex of this book);

—plan a trip to France, when it is possible;

—attend French events when there are some in your country or region;

—take some cooking classes online or within a group;

—and, of course, for the majority of our students, stick to their French lesson by Skype or Zoom at least once a week if possible.

Drawing up a specific list of tasks that you find important for you according to your way of learning or that you have decided to do on a regular basis because they fit with what you enjoy doing, whatever they are, is an excellent way to discipline oneself. It is too easy to be distracted, as we all know so well!

The pleasure of learning is fundamental to success

For us and all our teachers, this is one of the most satisfying aspects of giving French lessons: More than the progress our students make or the success they have, even more than the confidence they gain, it is when they tell us that they really enjoy studying the language. And indeed, most of the comments we get express this pleasure of learning. This is why making sure that our students have fun is a big part of our way of teaching — and it is much more enjoyable for us, too! If we start being bored teaching we will only ensure that our students will quickly give up...

This aspect of the learning process is even fundamental. If you do not take any pleasure in it, you miss one of the nicest parts of learning and everything will appear more difficult to you. Pleasure and good progress go hand in hand, and we would even say that if you're not enjoying yourself you will not go very far. One of our students, Blair Boone-Migura, a Non-profit Arts Director & University Instructor in New York and Hawaii, wrote recently: "Learn French at Home is truly a wonderful program and further proof that distance language learning is the modern way to go about studying language and culture. I am so pleased to have stumbled upon them after a simple Google search." And he adds: "a superb and stellar program... [for] any student looking to discover the exuberance and joy of the French language learning."

Therefore, one of the most important aspects in learning French is to be able to keep a balance between discipline and pleasure, motivation and coolness, work and fun. Well, isn't it the same for everything we do in life?

Keeping a sense of humor

Equally important is to keep one's sense of humor, as we already mentioned earlier. Laughing is one of the best ways to release tension. Most of our students noticed that when they can laugh with their teacher about something they find very difficult to understand or ridiculous (and it happens very often), this helps them a lot to memorize what they have laughed about. Our teachers' gentle and respectful sense of humor is considered as one of their best qualities.

During many of our lessons, we also like teaching our students a few jokes about strange French habits or some of the difficulties of the French language, such as this humorous remark from the American actor Steve Martin, quoted in *The New York Times*, that we particularly like: "Boy, those French! They have a different word for everything." And we regularly publish on our Facebook page funny short videos on learning French and good French jokes. We consider these examples of humor an important element of any pedagogical material!

TO REMEMBER FROM CHAPTER 5

• **Establish a daily or weekly routine for yourself.** Learning with a teacher, as indispensable as it is, is not sufficient. **Like all our students, try to find many other ways to practice your French,** such as reading an online newspaper, participating in social media groups, watching videos, meeting French people, etc.

• **Drawing up a specific list of tasks** is an excellent way to discipline yourself.

• The **pleasure of learning is fundamental to success.**

• **Pleasure and good progress** should go hand in hand.

• Don't forget to always **keep your sense of humor. Laughing** is one of the best ways **to release tension.**

6. LISTEN TO YOUR TEACHER, TO A SONG, WATCH A MOVIE...

AMONG THE LESSONS we can draw from our students experiences, and our own as their teachers, is the importance of listening to French in order to progress. It's essential if you want to get accustomed gradually to the pronunciation, understand much better any dialogue, enrich your vocabulary as well as pick up ways of expressing ideas or opinions. It will also help you being more comfortable and confident in speaking the language.

Learn to listen to your teacher

It stands to reason: Listening to your French teacher seems obvious. However, it happens quite often that you do not fully understand everything what the teacher is saying because you focus more on their attitude or the context of the explanation they give. Your teacher will probably realize it quite quickly and will take the time to explain in more simple terms — or in English if you are a beginner or if you prefer —what they were trying to tell you. If this doesn't happen, you should never hesitate to interrupt your teacher and simply say that you couldn't figure out what they were saying.

But even if you listen carefully to your teacher during each French lesson, this can never be enough. If you want to learn French, you have to avail yourself of as many opportunities as possible to listen to spoken French and work on your listening comprehension. All students should take full advantage of the many resources available on the internet. Below are a few suggestions.

Watch films, listen to the radio or podcasts...

Anything is worth listening to: news, sports events, ads, weather forecasts, game shows, short funny sketches, travel or literary programs, any good websites or ads with audio links, etc. This can be done almost anywhere, at anytime and is one of the main benefits of any type of smartphone or other device. You can take advantage of any "lost" time to listen to French as some of our students do.

We also recommend that you regularly watch French films and TV series (preferably with subtitles in French). Not only will that give you the chance to practice your listening comprehension but you will also be able to see and hear people speaking French between themselves. You can easily find such films on any streaming service.

A French film is also a perfect window to many aspects of French culture. Even if it is only "cinema" and obviously often exaggerated or contrived, it can give you a good picture of how the French react when faced with various situations, and also of the way they express their feelings. And it's a wonderful pastime! You'll find in our Annex our suggested list of good movies and series, most of which were recommended by our students.

Listening to French songs will help, too!

Listening to songs is another great tool for learning a language. The rhythm as well as the emotions expressed help you memorize the words. The voice of the singer also can be catchy. Listening to a French song is another way of learning more vocabulary, especially everyday expressions or very original idioms used by the singers.

Also, it tells you more than you may think about French culture and way of living.

Many students learning French are reluctant at first to try listening to French songs, fearing not to understand a word. But it's very easy to find the lyrics ("*les paroles*", in French) on the web. A French friend, or your teacher, can also explain to you the meaning of the song. You may very well love such an exercise. French songs tend to stick in our minds. Our students usually like it when their teachers have them listen to a song, before studying it and commenting on it together. It's also often a subject matter for a good discussion on the theme suggested by the song! Many of our students find it very instructive, and fun. It is the same with the readers of our free magazine, *French Accent*, in which we regularly publish French songs (with audio or video links and glossary).

One of our most productive and enjoyable activities in our immersion workshops is to have the participants watch the video of a song, fill in the blanks in a partially written version of the lyrics and then discuss the themes in the song.

The interest of our students for French songs also comes from their love of France, of its romantic appeal. Even more so than movies, French songs reflect perfectly the charm of France, and that is especially true for what we call *les chansons à texte*: ballads in which the lyrics play a major part, sometimes even more than the music itself. Many of these songs are also protest songs, or songs with a message which move the listeners and, frequently, have a certain influence on the French people and even on political figures. Such aspects are very interesting for a student who wants to immerse more into French culture. It is interesting to note that most of the songs created by the new generation still have this same type of romantic narratives as the older *chansons à texte*. We highly encourage you to forget about the classics and to discover new singers, and their beautiful ballades, as we do all the time in *French Accent Magazine*.

TO REMEMBER FROM CHAPTER 6

• When you listen, you learn.

• Learn to listen carefully to your teacher and never hesitate to have them repeat and explain what you haven't not understood.

• Watch French films, listen to the radio or podcasts. All of this is extremely useful to get used to the spoken French language and **an excellent and very pleasant way to immerse yourself in French culture.**

• **Listen to French songs** (*chansons à texte*) **and discover the French singers of the new generation.**

© DR

Steven: "I prefer old, classic French movies"

FOR ME, THE PROCESS OF LEARNING has centered on repetition and exposure to the language. I try to space out my lessons so that they are every other day, or every third day, on the days I don't have a lesson I am working independently, but I always try to have some French activity per day. Even while traveling, I try to maintain the pace of the lessons and studying. Most hotels have TV5Monde as a TV channel, which I find to be an excellent resource.

Each week I listen to News in Slow French, as well as try to watch at least one French movie. I prefer older, classic movies, and most of these have subtitles. At first, I used English subtitles, but I tried to quickly move to French subtitles. I hope to move away from using subtitles soon, to really focus on verbal language comprehension, which I have found challenging. Because the language is spoken slower in older movies, I spend a lot of time with movie reviews and reading ones I have found on French language film review sites.

"I always look up for words by myself during the lessons"

For each Learn French at Home lesson, I have a process that works well for me. I always review the materials from the last few lessons before, and then I spend time preparing for the lesson by having a French dictionary available, as well as a verb conjugation book. I also have a handwritten conjugation table for the common tenses of these verbs: *être, avoir, aller, faire,* and *devoir.* I am thinking of adding *devenir.* During the lesson, if I don't know or can't remember a verb conjugation, I always look it up myself, because that reinforces learning. I always look up a word I don't know in the dictionary for the same reason. I keep a website open during a lesson (Lawless French — subjunctivisor*) for on the go determination if a phrase requires the subjunctive, because I will remember better if I have to look it up myself.

"I review the words I had trouble pronouncing"

For the lesson, I come with a plan of things going on in my life that I would like to talk about, work, friends etc. For some lessons I will prepare a little presentation — anything that relates French to things important to me. After the lesson, I review the words I had trouble pronouncing, and any new vocabulary. I find reviewing it in the immediate time frame really helps with future accurate pronunciation.

I listen to News in Slow French once per week. I receive *France-Amérique* magazine, and I spend time reading the articles and working on the translation of the words I don't know. I also sent up TV5Monde alerts on my Facebook feed, so I receive a few of these during the day, and I practice my immediate comprehension abilities.

Steven Sorenson, M.D.
Diagnostic radiology specialist
Los Angeles, California, USA

_____

*www.lawlessfrench.com/subjunctivisor

Steven has been a student at Learn French at Home since 2019. Even though Steven has a very demanding profession, he will make sure that he has time for learning French and takes 3 to 4 lessons per week. Steven's French has improved considerably in just a few months. He makes a point of remembering what he learns by reinserting the vocabulary into different topics of conversation. Steven's French learning journey has been very rewarding on a weekly basis.

7. SPEAK FRENCH WITH THE FRENCH! THEY WILL LOVE IT

THERE IS NO REASON why you should wait until you understand French very well when reading it or listening to it to start speaking. On the contrary, as most of our students do, you shouldn't miss any opportunity to speak French, obviously with your teacher but also with French natives or Francophones as soon as you think you've mastered the basics. The best would be during a trip to France or a French-speaking country, but when it isn't possible on the occasion of a Zoom meeting or video conference or with French-speaking people you encounter in your city or region.

Take the initiative to speak French when you can!

This is what my Italian student Elena Valentini, who is a camp manager for a French NGO, did when she was still on lockdown it Italy and had to have meetings with colleagues in Africa before she could join them on the continent. She felt bad because most briefings and webinars used to take place in English and she knew that it was very difficult for many of her Francophile colleagues who weren't fluent in English. So, she took the initiative to organize and manage a webinar in French, in which some 40 people participated.

Elena was quite apprehensive at the beginning. She had already chaired a few Zoom meetings in French. The first one was very stressful for her. Just after, she told me: "When I was asked the first question, I was suddenly speechless, my head was empty, I didn't know what to say. Then I took a deep breath and I was able to answer." And after that she expressed herself perfectly well in French during the whole meeting, and the following ones. It was a good training for the webinar, that she managed perfectly well! She told me she was so relieved and pleased when she sent me the link for the webinar. I listened to it and was really impressed. I warmly congratulated her. It was also very satisfying for me as her teacher that she had gained such confidence.

Practice with your teacher

The first person with whom you'll speak French is obviously your teacher. But it isn't enough to exchange a few words and then work on a specific text which you are already familiar with. You need to engage in "real life" conversations similar to those you'll have when you'll speak with a French native. This is an important part of our work. During their lessons, all the teachers of *Learn French at Home* always try to help their students get ready by creating role plays adapted to the situation they may encounter. We also make sure that the students know very well how to introduce themselves and are familiar with the customary expressions used by the French when they meet someone for the first time. Such conversational formulas are also reproduced in our books and we encourage our students to listen to the audio links attached to the eBook versions and to repeat them over and over again.

The more you feel confident speaking naturally with your teacher, the easier it will be to do the same with other French natives.

The French will react positively

When you think you are ready, it will be time to take the plunge and start trying out your speaking skills with French people. You have to know that most people with whom you dare to take the first step and begin a conversation with will react very positively and be ready to help. This is why you should not hesitate to talk to French people that you may encounter during your trips to France, or to people you have the opportunity to meet in your country or through a screen! You'll be surprised how positively responsive they can be. They are not going to judge you negatively because you are speaking French to them; most probably, they'll be pleasantly surprised, will find you courageous and perhaps they might even be a bit amused.

Either way, you will gain respect and admiration from them, as they very rarely appreciate people who systematically address them in English (the French may even feel insulted when someone addresses them only in English without even saying *Bonjour*). They will be very happy that you're making the effort to use their language with them, even if you cannot say more than a few words.

How to break the ice

The French have a reputation for answering or addressing people (foreigners or other French) with frank remarks and some rudeness. Quite often, such a cold attitude at the beginning is caused by some kind of shyness on their part. However, if you make the effort to speak their language, not forgetting to smile, they will soon be much nicer. Equally if not more important is, as we said above, to have started any conversation or question, even in a store, a bar, a bus, under any and every circumstance by the indispensable *Bonjour* or, even better, *Bonjour Madame, Bonjour Monsieur...* And when you leave, it's nice and appreciated if you say *Au revoir !*

You should also not worry at all about annoying, insulting or embarrassing anyone. If you think or realize you made a blunder, just add expressions such as *pardon, je suis désolé(e), excusez-moi* (various ways to say: I am sorry, excuse me). When you ask something it is always nice to say *s'il vous plaît* (please). And of course you should never forget to say *merci* or even *merci beaucoup* (thanks a lot).

Don't be ashamed of your accent!

Most people consider foreign accents appealing and charming while they hate listening to their own accent when they try expressing themselves in a foreign language! You will be surprised to realize that the French really like your accent when you speak French to them. The French themselves have very different accents whether they come from Bretagne, Alsace, the Massif Central or Provence and they are used to the Quebec, Swiss and Belgian accents.

A useful tip to improve your pronunciation

In each issue of our free magazine *French Accent*, that you can download on any device and in most of the eBook version of our publications, you'll find several audio links. Each time you click on one of them, you open a webpage on which you can listen to the text to which an audio link in linked. It is usually a glossary or another kind of list of words and/or expressions, a poem, a song, several French-English scenarios and the full text of all our short stories read in French.

We advise our readers not only to listen to these audio files but to practice repeating out loud what they hear, and doing so several times until they feel confident that their pronunciation is almost as good as what they hear. Of course, ideally, it is better if they can repeat them in front of a French person or with their teacher who can correct them. This is an excellent exercise to help you improve your spoken French — and also, almost as important, to help you memorize these words and expressions that you have learned. This is why repeating out loud is a good habit to adopt.

TO REMEMBER FROM CHAPTER 7

• **You should not miss any opportunity to speak French with French-speaking people, or even take the initiative!**

• **Practice as much as possible with your teacher.** The more you feel confident speaking naturally with them, the easier it will be to do the same with other French natives.

• **The French will react positively if you address them in their language.** As long as you say *bonjour* and you smile...

• **Learn how to break the ice** when you address French people.

• **Don't be ashamed of your accent!**

• **A useful tip to improve your pronunciation: Listen to the audio links in our magazine and eBooks and repeat out loud** every word and sentence.

8. A FEW TIPS ON HOW TO ADDRESS FRENCH PEOPLE

HOW TO START A CONVERSATION, how to ask questions, how to explain in a simple way what you want to say to a French person...? Here are a few basic tips that should help you.

Say *vous* instead of *tu*

When you encounter any French-speaking adult, unless they are a friend or a child, you should definitely think of using "*vous*" instead of "*tu*" if you want to avoid finding yourself in an embarrassing situation.

Asking questions: the easier way

In French, you have several ways of asking questions. The more traditional, and the less used, it to invert the subject and the verb:
— *Parlez-vous anglais ?* (Do you speak English?)
    Another possible interrogative form, which is more common, but that some students find more difficult, is to add "*est-ce que*" before the subject + verb + noun/adjective:
— *Est-ce que vous parlez anglais ?*
    But there is another and easier way that the French use all the time between themselves. You can simply use a normal word order

(subject + verb + noun) followed by a question mark and rising intonation at the end:

—*Vous parlez anglais ?*

Here is another example, with an interrogative adverb: If you are about to take a train at a French station and are not sure of its destination, you want to say: Where is it going? There are three ways to ask this in French:

—*Où va-t-il ?* (adverb + verb + subject).

—*Où est-ce qu'il va ?* (adverb + *est-ce que* + subject + verb).

—*Il va où ?* (subject + verb + adverb). This is the easier way and, again, this is the one most French people use.

To make it easy, make it short

When speaking with French people face to face or on a screen, instead of trying to translate exactly in French the sentence you'd use in English, try to find an easier and shorter way to express yourself. Instead of trying to make long sentences, make them short, replace a difficult phrase by an easier one, go straight to the point. This will be better received by the French person to whom you are trying to say something than in using long and complicated explanations.

For example, if someone asks you where and for how long you have been studying French, try to avoid complicated explanations and simply summarize your experience. Instead of saying: *J'ai suivi des cours de français à l'école pendant deux ans quand j'étais jeune, avant de reprendre des leçons par Zoom en avril dernier.* = I have been taking French lessons at school for two years when I was young, before having more lessons by Zoom last April, why don't you just say: *J'ai appris le français à l'école et j'ai repris par Zoom en avril.* = I learned French at school, and I've started again by Zoom in April.

The art of avoiding the subjunctive

For most of our students the subjunctive is a nightmare and often, even if they've managed to master it, they completely forget how it is formed when they talk to a French person. If you find yourself in this position, don't panic. There is always another way to formulate what you want to say: to use the infinitive or a noun instead. Note also that you can always shorten your sentence to make it easier, as shown in the example below:

You are invited by a French person for dinner but you already have a commitment for the evening (or you don't feel ready to spend a full evening speaking French). If you want to decline the invitation and say something like: "I am sorry, but I can't, I have to go to the train station this evening," you would say, using the subjunctive: *Je suis désolé(e), mais ce n'est pas possible, il faut que j'aille à la gare ce soir*. An easier way is using the infinitive: *Je suis désolé(e), mais c'est* pas possible, je dois aller à la gare ce soir*. Or you can simply say, with a smile: *Merci beaucoup mais désolé(e), je dois aller à la gare*.

The French, too, make mistakes!

As we already said, you should not think that you are the only one to make mistakes, far from it. Sometimes, when we receive the homework from our students, it happens that we are surprised by the few mistakes they make compared to what many French people do in letters, emails or any postings on social media.

As most of the communication in France is done by email or other quick and easy ways of communication, and as very few people take the time to read and correct what they write, this explains — partly — why there are so many mistakes in such exchanges. One of the most usual errors is the confusion between the infinitive and the past participle. For example, we often read something like: *On a bien travailler*, instead of *On a bien travaillé* (We have done a good job).

For a foreigner who starts to have a rather good knowledge of French it is a little reassuring and it may even be really fun to see so many mistakes made by French people!

In texts, chats, tweets, posts on Instagram, Facebook... another type of French!

Exactly like in English, most people write just phonetically when they use any of these new ways of communication. It seems even like a game, some apparent errors are made intentionally to make such communication more fun. And this is also a way for the French people to avoid a few difficulties of their language that they find annoying when they write on their smartphones, particularly the circumflex accent or the cedilla on the letter "c" or the apostrophes, the double consonants, the mute vowels at the end of words, etc. As much as they can, they simply shorten the words.

Here are a few examples of contractions or transformations of words:

—**c toi**, instead of *c'est toi* (is that you);

—**sava ?**, instead of *ça va ?* (are you OK?);

—**y a**, or **ya**, instead of *il y a* (there is);

—**HT**, instead of *acheter* (to buy);

—**pasque**, instead of *parce que* (because);

—**paré**, instead of *il paraît* (it seems);

—**a12c4**, instead of *à un de ces quatre* (see you soon);

—**ta la dal ?**, instead of *tu as la dalle ?* (are you hungry? — in slang);

—**aPro**, instead of *apéro* (aperitive).

---

*Note that in spoken French the "*ne*" (first part of the negative) is very often dropped.

TO REMEMBER FROM CHAPTER 8

A few hints to help you deal with the main difficulties you will encounter when speaking with French people:

● **Prefer** *vous* **instead of** *tu.*

● **How to ask questions** might also be a difficulty but there are easier ways, that the French use all the time.

● **To make it easy, make it short.** It will be so much easier to communicate what you want to say by using short sentences.

● **How to avoid using the subjunctive.**

● Again, **don't forget that French people make mistakes too** — a lot of them.

● They also have **funny ways of communicating by text, chat, tweets, etc.**

Ann: "I enjoy reading mystery novels that feature a lot of dialogue"

LEARN FRENCH AT HOME has been a part of my life since 2016, when I began taking weekly lessons with Céline; by 2017 I felt confident enough to move to Lyon, France, where my husband Mark and I now live; and he's a LFAH student too!

But while it's absolutely necessary to work with a teacher in a structured manner, I've found that *truly* learning French takes more than lessons alone.

When we arrived in France three years ago, I could see that in order to get up to speed I'd have

© DR

to add a lot to my learning arsenal, and that the more I knew about French culture, the easier it would be to learn and retain the language.

So, here is what I do in addition to continuing with my weekly lessons: We buy the local newspaper every day and I get local news alerts on my phone (in French of course); I also subscribe to magazines about art and other subjects I enjoy, and I've changed the base language on my phone to French. I follow several French-language Instagram and Twitter accounts,

especially about Lyon and about museums and other cultural insti-
tutions here in France. To improve my reading comprehension and
vocabulary, I read (fairly) easy French books and use them as a
springboard for my LFAH lessons; I particularly enjoy light
mystery novels that feature lots of dialogue.

To improve my spoken French and comprehension, I have a conversation partner who helps me with French as I help her with
English, and I belong to a few conversation groups that include
native French speakers. Mark and I keep up with the news and
are sure to watch important speeches on TV from President
Macron and others.

"Improving my French
has become a major part of my life"

Just recently I've started doing easy crossword puzzles and
playing other word games in French. Needless to say I have a
huge feeling of accomplishment whenever I successfully complete a "*jeu de mots*." We watch French films on television and
have a French classical-music radio station on most of the day. I
also take comprehension quizzes on TV5Monde, and have pur-
chased several online video lessons from *Comme Une Française*,
which focuses on French culture and everyday life.

"The French are very proud of their cultural history"

In the evenings, my husband and I sometimes play French trivia
board games: the French are very proud of their cultural history
and like to show it off in all sorts of ways. And finally, since we
live in France, I practice my French every day as I make my
shopping rounds.

I'm sure there's even more that I haven't even thought of — improving my French has become a major part of my life. All the things I do to practice French feed into my weekly lessons, so I've been making great progress since we arrived in Lyon. I plan to continue my lessons because they give me the structure I enjoy, and that I need to stay on track.

Ann Bingley Gallops
Former Feng Shui Consultant
Lyon, France

Ann has been a student at Learn French at Home since 2016. Ann fulfilled her dream in moving with her husband to France after making sure that her level of French was sufficient enough to enjoy the day to day living. Ann works hard at learning French; she sets clear objectives with her French learning and always reaches them. Her French learning journey has been very impressive and today she's able to fully appreciate her life in France.

9. GET IN THE HABIT OF READING, ANYTHING

READING FRENCH IS AMONG the necessary things you've to do when you start learning the language. You don't need to start with Molière or Rousseau, reading anything you can find, and they are plethora on the web, will help you familiarize with written French: short news articles, blogs, sports reviews, Facebook posts, titles or photo captions or even ads. And when you've have reached an intermediate or advanced level, reading books or booklets in French with the use of a dictionary is definitely an excellent habit. It will be a challenge and it doesn't matter if you only understand a small percentage of it, but you'll be very proud when you'll be able to read a full book!

A unique asset of Learn French at Home: our books

Learn French at Home publishes a unique and wide variety of unique French learning books and books of fiction with audio at a very reasonable price. For most of them, you can choose between the eBook version (pdf), which will allow you to listen to the audio links (glossaries, scenarios, short stories in full, etc.) and the paperback. And if you purchase the paperback version, available on Amazon in several countries, there is a link to get the eBook version for free.

Our best-seller is our *French Grammar Basics and Beyond*, which is totally unique as it contains very simple explanations of French grammar rules in English and numerous exercises with solutions. It has been recognized as indispensable by our students who all use it. Our students find extremely useful some of the other books that are very specific, such as *Traveling in France*, when they visit Paris or various regions of France. There is also a book conceived for kids with games, *Learn French with Fun Activities*, that was a particularly big success with parents doing homeschooling during the long periods of confinement!

Short stories with a surprise ending

Our books that our intermediate and advanced students like the most are those in a series of captivating short stories with a surprising twist at the end. They are accompanied by glossaries, grammar tips, cultural notes, exercises (solutions at the end) and full audio. Four such books (eBooks and paperback versions) have already been published. They not only enhance the readers' understanding of the language and the culture but they give them pleasure in reading accessible French literature. More details on page 127.

French Accent Magazine: a very useful free tool

Since we started it in 2006, we have published nearly 90 issues of our *French Accent Magazine* (pdf format), every 2 months. In 2019, we decided to make it available free of charge so that it could help a larger number of French learners. We highly encourage you to subscribe to it. The articles, written in French for the most part, with French glossaries, scenarios and audio links, cover many aspects of French society and culture. It always starts with an excellent article on grammar or communication, explained in English.

To subscribe: www.learnfrenchathome.com/french-accent-magazine

Why not try French literature?

As soon as you feel comfortable enough or encouraged by your teacher who will give you the best advice on the books you could start with, you'll discover what reading French literature can bring to a person who is learning the language. It is through literature that you can find the very deepest expressions of those emotions found in every situation in life, and it is also in literature that you can appreciate better how the French people react to these emotions or to the events that provoked them.

Studying French literature is one of the best entryways to French culture. That may also be the case for good French essays, biographies, history books, etc. as long as they are well written and interesting. You'll have to get used to an aspect of French literature that most students anticipate with apprehension: *le passé simple*, a tense in which so many verbs are conjugated in books. It may seem difficult at first but it is used exactly in the same context as *le passé composé*, that most intermediate students master very well. You'll quickly get used to it — and relieved to know that you'll never need to write or say anything in the *passé simple* in your communication in French!

When you make your choice, it's best to start with books that aren't too difficult! To avoid needless frustration, try not to be too ambitious. In the Annex of this book, we give a few suggestions of books that our students like and recommend.

TO REMEMBER FROM CHAPTER 9

• **Read as much as you can, and anything**: newspaper articles, blogs, books or booklets, etc. or even ads.

• Discover the **unique collection of French learning books** published by Learn French at Home. Among them, **an extremely useful grammar book with easy explanations in English and exercises** (with corrections), **which is our best-seller.**

• Our students and readers like a lot our **series of short suspense stories** with grammar tips, exercises and audio.

• **Subscribe to our very useful tool, totally free:** *French Accent Magazine.*

• **Why not try French literature?** It is in literature that you can **appreciate better how the French people react** in many situations. Literature is also one of **the best entry-ways to French culture.**

10. WRITE IN FRENCH, YOU'LL MAKE IT WITH SOME HELP

VERY FEW FREE LEARNING programs or websites you may be using to learn vocabulary, basic grammar or expressions will allow you to practice writing with good feedback and corrections that will help you to make progress. It is not something you can really do on your own. Yet, this is a very important aspect of learning, even if you are studying French only to be able to talk to French people or if you think you'll never need to write much.

By knowing how to write, you can gain a much better knowledge not only of the language but of the way to express yourself in French, which is different than in English. And it's also a good way to use the grammar rules that you've learned and to feel comfortable doing it.

To be able to write in French, even if only emails, you'll need help. Some French friends may be able to help you but they may hesitate or be reluctant to correct your mistakes, your grammar and to tell you exactly how a French person would have written it. This is why it is important that you get the help of a good French teacher. Writing will be part of the homework they'll give you.

Homework is crucial

Homework, which is an integral part of any course of study, will help you improve your writing. As it isn't usually something you can do during a lesson, writing exercises are often part of any well-prepared and useful homework.

However, when you speak of homework, the first thoughts that cross the minds of many people are: homework is difficult, is annoying, takes too much time, is not focused enough on what I need, is useless, etc. But this is true only if your teacher is making it boring or if you aren't motivated enough to work by yourself outside of the lessons... Assigning homework and correcting your exercises has nothing to do with any sadistic motivation by their teacher to make you suffer, and it is at least as demanding for the teacher as it is for you. While a student is supposed to have an hour and a half homework assignment, their teacher may easily spend the same amount of time, if not more, in preparing and correcting it. At least this is what happens with all our teachers at Learn French at Home. As it is the case for any lesson, the homework given by our teachers is totally adapted to the students' goals and proficiency level and also to what they feel comfortable in doing. It is just a matter of common sense: If the homework is made too difficult, it will discourage the students and will not teach them anything.

At Learn French at Home, the homework is very personalized. Most exercises are created by the teachers on subjects of interest to the students and use grammar rules, vocabulary and idiomatic expressions they might particularly want to learn. The teachers use many of our publications to help answer the particular needs and questions from the students, such as *French Accent Magazine*. All teachers also use a selection of textbooks and a wide range of online material to facilitate understanding.

When a teacher patiently corrects you

For every written assignment or short translation of a text from English to French, you'll appreciate having a French native teacher who patiently corrects you, takes the time to explain the various ways a French person would have written it, suggests a few common expressions you could use, reminds you of a few grammar rules, helps you be aware of the little problems of agreements in the feminine form or the plural, the placement of an adjective or adverb, etc.

A very good way to discuss together your writing project through Skype or Zoom is to do a screen sharing. Then your teacher makes all comments and corrections literally before your eyes. After the lesson, the teacher will send you by email the corrected text so that you can read it again and memorize it better.

Again, all this process is done in a very relaxed way with humor and positive feedback and it can lead to very interesting discussions afterwards. It's a good way to have our students love their homework!

Les dictées

In each issue of *French Accent Magazine*, we publish two *dictées* (dictations), one for beginners, one for intermediate and advanced learners. They appear in the first pages, with audio links you can listen to while trying to write them down. The texts are reproduced in the last part of the magazine, with the links again, so that you can listen to them one more time while comparing your transcription to the original text.

When homework makes a difference

All our teachers say that they see the difference between students who regularly do their homework and those who don't. They can see a clear progression.

Doing your homework is also a demonstration of your motivation, it stimulates your interest and it is fundamental for absorbing what has been covered in the lesson.

Some students prefer doing their homework right after their lesson to make sure not to forget what they have learned. Others do it just before the next one as a way of getting ready for the lesson, and some other students work on it a little every day. No matter how you do your homework, it always helps to improve your knowledge and understanding and is an important reinforcement of what you have learned.

TO REMEMBER FROM CHAPTER 10

• Even if you don't intend to write in French very often, **writing is an important part of your study** and is difficult to do on you own if you have nobody to help and correct you.

• **Homework is a crucial part of the French learning process** and an exercise that will help you improve your writing.

• **You need a good teacher patiently correcting you and helping you write like a French person would,** through screen sharing for example.

• **Listening to our *dictées* and trying to write them is a fun way to learn!**

• **Homework can really make a difference**, as we know very well from experience.

Hrant: "I acquired the 'habit' of making French friends"

I STARTED LEARNING French through the Alliance Française, taking 1-2 classes a week. But I quickly realized that, even with homework, weekly classes were not enough to progress as quickly as I wanted. So, for a couple of years, I complemented the classes with podcasts such as Coffee Break French (which comes with teaching material) and News in Slow French. I then started to take private classes in person with Learn French At Home. I still maintain the weekly sessions at the Alliance (now through Zoom), but these are now conversation classes.

My main learning habit consists of speaking French with people whenever possible, whether I'm traveling in France or just socializing with people I know. You could say I acquired the "habit" of making French friends. As habits go, it's not such a bad one, but it can be addictive.

Various teachers have become friends, so that social activities either with them or with other students have introduced me to even more speakers. At work, several colleagues are French, and they were all willing to speak with me. I found out that they didn't mind my awkward French — I just needed to get over the fear of making mistakes.

In addition to my regular lessons I have read several books and I enjoy watching French movies or TV series. The books take a while because I look up all the vocabulary that I don't know, but it's a great way to learn. Movies are less straightforward because they tend to include more slang and one has to keep up with the fast pace of a natural conversation. I have at times watched a movie twice (e.g. *Le Prénom*), once with English subtitles to make sure I understand the story, and then again with French subtitles so I can understand any dialogue which is too fast for me in real-time.

"I accepted to give tours in French in a museum"

I volunteer as a guide at a museum in Houston, and on two occasions I was asked to give a 1-hour tour in French. At first I resisted, because it forced me to use the language in a completely different way: instead of a normal conversation, I now had to explain concepts in art or history, requiring different vocabulary and a different way of expressing oneself. But it turned out to be a great experience!

Hrant Yardumian
Software Engineer
Houston, USA

Hrant has been a student at Learn French at Home since 2016. Every week, he looks forward to working on his French and has always been a curious and inquisitive student. He's always supplemented the lessons with some fun French activities, and today Hrant is able to speak at an advanced level on any topics, and can even joke in French.

11. YES, YOU'LL HAVE A FEW HURDLES TO OVERCOME: OUR TIPS TO DEAL WITH THEM

THE FRENCH LANGUAGE HAS SINGULAR particularities that challenge many people. Here are a few of them and how to deal with them, or to simply not feel bad about them.

The gender of nouns: a permanent question mark

This is the case with the gender of nouns. You have to accept that you'll always be puzzled wondering whether a word is masculine or feminine and you will never know it perfectly! It's one of the major differences between English and French and it drives many of our students crazy, especially as there are just not precise rules about it!

If many words ending in "*e*" are feminine, a lot of others are masculine, such as *groupe* (group), *verre* (glass), *problème* (problem), *silence* (silence), *parapluie* (umbrella), or even *féminisme* (feminism). Sometimes bigger things are masculine and smaller ones feminine, as is the case for *camion* (truck, m.) and *voiture* (car, f.), but *une grue* (a construction crane), which is much bigger than a truck, is, feminine... For many words, there is simply no logical explanation. For example, why is *malheur* (misfortune) masculine and *peur* (fear) feminine?

The only way to avoid making too many mistakes is to try to memorize the most common words. This will take time, but several of our students have told us than after a few months of paying attention to what they read and hear, they see an improvement. And sometimes you can cheat by using the plural, which avoids being wrong! The British actress Jane Birkin could never remember that the word *baguette* is feminine. So, instead of hesitating between *un* or *une baguette* when she is in a boulangerie she asks for *deux baguettes*... A solution that might be costly, though, depending on what you want to purchase!

In any case, you should never feel bad about it. Even senior Francophiles living in France, who have been speaking French for many years and master the grammar often better than some French people, still make mistakes with the gender of nouns that a 6 year-old French child would not make. Do not take too much time or trouble with such typical errors. The French will always understand what you mean. They won't criticize you or make fun of you, they will just find it amusing and cute.

The accent marks: tricky but important to know

At first glance, if may not seem very important to know very well where to put the accents on French words. However, if you do not properly use them, not only will you make a mistake while writing in French but your pronunciation could very well be wrong. The same word can also have a totally different meaning depending on the accent placed on one vowel. For example: *prés* (fields) and *près* (close to), *mais* (but) and *maïs* (corn), *cote* (popularity) and *côte* (coast), or *sur* (above) and *sûr* (certain). It is also very important to be aware of the role of accent marks in verb conjugations. They affect the pronunciation of the verb. For example with the verb *espérer* (to hope): *j'espère, nous espérons* (I hope, we hope).

The best solution to overcome this difficulty is to memorize these accent marks (there are not so many after all) and to learn how to pronounce them. Your teacher will help you and you'll find many examples, with audio, in our books and our magazine and in most websites or apps for learning French that you can listen to in order to learn how to pronounce the words with accent marks.

The nasal vowels, another snag

Equally difficult is to assimilate the pronunciation of the nasal vowels: "*en*," "*in*," "*on*," "*un*" and some other vowel combinations ("*eu*," "*ou*," etc.) — or, worse, groups of vowels and consonants such as "*aille*" or "*ouille*."

It takes some time to get it, but you should not get too stressed about it and try to make it a fun exercise when you attempt to pronounce some of the more problematic words, such as *moyen* (average), *champignon* (mushroom), *pneu* (tyre), *broussaille* (bushes), or *grenouille* (frog). Doing phonetic exercises with your teacher is often the occasion for a good laugh!

Choosing a preposition is like playing the lottery

The use of prepositions in French, as with other languages, can be very frustrating and it is an ongoing process to learn which preposition to use after particular expressions or verbs. You simply have to memorize them as you go along. For example, in English we say: "to listen <u>to</u> something," whereas in French there is no preposition used after the verb *écouter*; we also look at something "<u>on</u> television," while in French it is "<u>à</u> (at) *la télévision*," etc. Also, in French, the preposition can be different for the same verb depending on its meaning: We say *décider <u>de</u> faire quelque chose* (to decide to do something) and *se décider <u>à</u>* (to make up one's mind).

Again, don't worry too much about it, all students are in the same boat and the French won't pay much attention, if any at all, to such tiny mistakes.

Pronouns: Which ones to use? Where to put them?

This aspect of the French grammar is probably one of the most complex, and it usually takes a long time for a student to perfectly assimilate the various pronouns and their placement in a sentence. It is, however, important that you learn the rules for each specific pronoun. For example direct and indirect object pronouns are always placed before the verb. We say "I love you" in English, but, as everybody knows, it is *je t'aime* in French.

Your teacher will have you work on it and you should never hesitate to ask your French friends for help in case you aren't sure which one to use when chatting with them. You'll be very proud the day you'll be able to use the right pronoun in a sentence.

The conjugation of verbs

Conjugating the verbs and especially the numerous irregular ones is also not the easiest part of learning French. Most of our students find particularly discouraging the fact that there are several conjugations to use in the past — especially the *passé simple* as we said earlier. And it takes a long time to get used to the subjunctive, too!

In *French Accent Magazine*, we have published many articles on the various conjugations, explained in clear terms. For all our teachers, helping you mastering the most commonly used conjugations is an important part of their work and of the homework they'll give you. All our students get it over time.

Learning idiomatic French expressions is really fun

For our students, it's among the best parts at learning French! Indeed, it may be the most interesting and amusing aspect of the French language and a very important one, too. The French use so many idiomatic expressions in their daily language, together with many little words that do not always have a very specific meaning, that if you do not know the most common ones you may be completely lost and unable to understand a very simple dialogue between two French people! We place a lot of importance on commonly used idiomatic expressions in every issue of *French Accent Magazine*. See more on such expressions on page 107.

Vulgar or not vulgar?

This is a very difficult question that all our students ask one day or another. When learning French words idiomatic expressions, some of them are a bit shocked by the words used and they don't know if they could really repeat them without insulting the people with whom they speak. They also wonder if these tricky expressions are currently used by everybody or only by less educated people. This is definitely a sensitive subject. How to determine which ones are vulgar, or rude? Some words are so commonly used that nobody notices them anymore, and most French people have even forgotten their original meaning. A good example is *putain*, which literally means "pros-titute" but that most French women and men invariably use to express almost every feeling and its contrary: surprise, enthusiasm, joy, disappointment, anger, pain, sadness. But some others are undeniably a little vulgar. We've published several articles about such touchy vocabulary. Your teacher will be the best person to tell you what's acceptable or not, especially for a foreigner. Before using any such word or expression you've read or heard, you should never be shy to ask your teacher about them!

It is the same for the subject of love and personal relationships, an important aspect of French culture. We've also tackled the subject several times and we will continue to do so.

However if, out of ignorance, you curse or use a swear word that will immediately appear inappropriate, no need to say "Pardon my French!" Not a single French person will understand what you mean. It is better not to worry. It is more than likely that the French person who listens to you hides a smile — or tells you kindly in simple words a way to say the same thing a little differently.

TO REMEMBER FROM CHAPTER 11

Here are some of our tips to overcome the most common hurdles you will certainly encounter:

• **The gender of nouns: Try to memorize the most common words.** After some time and practice you will make fewer mistakes. And **don't worry about it,** the French will understand you anyway and will even find it cute!

• **The accent marks and the nasal vowels: Practice a lot with your teacher and with audio links** on websites and on our publications.

• **The prepositions and pronouns: Studying French grammar** will be very useful to know how to use them. If you don't know which ones to use when speaking, **don't hesitate to ask French people for advice.**

• **The conjugation of verbs:** This is another reason why **studying grammar and having a teacher is essential.** Also very helpful will be **to carefully read our grammar articles** in *French Accent Magazine* and our other publications, in which **all explanations are given in English.**

• **Idiomatic expressions:** The French use a multitude of them, some very funny. This is one of **the most interesting and amusing aspect of the French language! Try to learn a few of them on a regular basis,** pay attention to **the context** in which you can use them and **to those that might appear inappropriate... or definitely vulgar.**

12. DISCOURAGED? IT HAPPENS, AND IT'S NO BIG DEAL

IT HAPPENS TO MOST STUDENTS. One day, after a few months or years of studying French, you suddenly have the feeling that you aren't making any more progress, that you have reached a plateau and that you are stuck there. It is important to prepare yourself for it. We could simply say: Do not accept that you're in a rut and move forward, there is no doubt that you'll soon get over it.

We also know that it may be easier said than done. Below are a few suggestions on how to get through this difficult stage.

Stop, take the time to reflect, talk to your teacher

The first thing to do when you are faced with any strong feeling of frustration or discouragement is to acknowledge it, accept it and reflect on it. Why do you have this feeling? Is it true that you are stuck at a plateau?

If you take the time to observe the progress you have made since the beginning, you may on the contrary realize that you have learned a lot already, that you feel much more confident speaking or writing, that you understand better what French people tell you. You should tell your teacher about your doubts or frustrations. Your teacher is the person who knows how you've progressed over the months and will probably be able, more than you, to assess your level and to confirm with concrete examples how you've evolved, what you've already learned and memorized, etc.

Acknowledge what you have already assimilated

Then, you could look back at your initial objectives and take the time to observe in depth what you have achieved already. This will certainly make you realize that you've learned much more than you think. The simple fact of reviewing your personal objectives might be enough to give you the motivation to continue. Would it not be too bad to have reached this stage and not keep on going?

We know very well from experience than such a phase of discouragement is just a temporary one. Ups and downs are typical of any undertaking in life. This is a phase you'll probably all go through and there is no doubt that, even if you are not totally aware of it, you are indeed moving forward towards your goals.

There is no such thing as reaching a point where you no longer move ahead. Many grammar rules, vocabulary or expressions that you haven't fully absorbed along the way will come back to you naturally when it is time, when you are ready to assimilate them. Do not let this feeling of discouragement take over your initial enthusiasm. Mistakes and obstacles are part of the experience of learning a language. Learning French is not that easy, and you have every reason to be very proud of your achievements. Remember also the joy you've encountered at each step of your progress and acknowledge what you've already assimilated.

Take a break

It goes for language learning as for any undertaking in life. When you have the feeling that you are overwhelmed or that you are totally stuck and feel that you are not making any progress, why not close your French textbook, tell your teacher that you are taking one or two weeks break and just think about something else for a little while? There is no need at all to approach a state of burn-out by being too obstinate or insisting on going too fast when you obviously cannot devote enough time to your study or you feel discouraged because you won't be fluent as soon as you were anticipating. Provided that this break doesn't last too long, it might regenerate you, give you the impetus you were missing and it may also very well help you realize the progress you've already made. You will then be able to go back to studying with a relaxed and more positive attitude.

Also, taking a break and giving yourself all the time you need to relax and pamper yourself is typical of the French way of thinking! As you certainly know, resting, napping, taking long weekends and vacations are important priorities for all French people, therefore your French teacher will certainly understand you when you feel the need for it!

Don't give up and get back on track!

Now that you have realized the progress you have made since you started, that you understand that there is no such point where you remain stuck, that learning can only be progressive, that you constantly evolve even if you aren't always aware of it, and that you have taken the time to take some rest and to recharge your batteries, you'll certainly have regained the energy and willpower that you had at the beginning. You've lost confidence temporarily, but think what you'd lose if you quit altogether. Think of your objectives, of the reasons why you wanted to learn French or improve your knowledge and move forward! After this phase of discouragement, and a little break, you may have more energy when you get back on track and even learn more quickly!

TO REMEMBER FROM CHAPTER 12

You may very well feel a little discouraged at a certain point. You have the feeling that you've reached a plateau and you are stuck there. **Here are our suggestions on how to overcome this very natural feeling.**

• **Stop, take the time to reflect and talk to your teacher about your doubts and frustrations.** Your teacher is the one who knows best how you've evolved.

• **Acknowledge what you have already assimilated — much more than you think.** And remember that there is no such thing as reaching a point where you no longer move ahead.

• Don't forget that **mistakes and obstacles are inevitably part of the experience of learning a language.**

• **Remember the joy you have encountered** at each step of your progress.

• **Take a (short) break and relax, the French way!**

• **Don't give up and move on as soon that you have re-charged your batteries!**

Patti: "I learn a lot by reading novels in French"

I BELIEVE MY APPROACH to learning French as a second language has helped me retain what I learn. Because I am a morning person, I take advantage of that quiet time to work on French. Each day I listen to something in French, be it a French film, French radio, or a YouTube video in French. These are not how-to-learn-French videos, but news videos or travelogues that use every day French language.

In addition, I am reading a book in French. I prefer novels, but I often read non-fiction too. In the beginning, I had a dictionary at hand to define words I did not know, but soon I ignored it and determined meaning by context. Now I am fairly fluent with my reading, and I can truly enjoy the story. I believe I learn a lot by reading French — especially new vocabulary and verb conjugation.

I also truly enjoy challenging homework given to me by my teacher. I often research the subtleties of the lesson so I can discern the particulars of usage. If my teacher gives me an article, I often research the people and history behind it, to give me a deeper understanding of French culture. Writing in French is important too. I learn new vocabulary when I am searching for that particular verb that expresses what I

© DR

want to say. For me, writing helps me remember, and I will hand-write my homework before I type it for my teacher. That repetition allows me to find mistakes I may have made, as well as give me one more time to mechanically fix things in my brain.

"My dog likes to hear me read out loud!"

It is important to speak. In addition to my regular class, I have scheduled conversations two times a week for practice. I believe this has helped me a lot. I also find time to read aloud. I think it is beneficial to make my mouth form the words. I am glad my dog likes to hear me read out loud!

Because I am a high school teacher, I like to model the act of studying for my students. I will often tell them what I am learning, discuss a particular challenge, and ask them for ideas or opinions about an issue for my writing. I know this seems like a lot to do, and one does not have to do all of it every day; however, I believe this type of dedication makes a difference. Find a teacher who will support you in your endeavors, and you will grow with French!

Patricia Pattison
High School Teacher
Port Angeles, Washington, USA

Patti is passionate about learning French. She has been a student at Learn French at Home since 2017. She works hard and is determined to master the language. She is not afraid to tackle and learn the more advanced grammar points. She will spend hours on a weekly basis and has acquired a very large vocabulary bank. Patti can speak and debate about any subjects in French.

13. PRACTICE: ESSENTIAL IF YOU WANT TO MAKE IT HAPPEN

PRACTICE, PRACTICE, PRACTICE again is essential when you want to learn a language, or anything. All throughout this book, we have stressed this need to practice on your own, constantly. As fundamental as your French lessons are, they will never be sufficient unless you practice almost everyday! Here are a few tips on how to do it in an efficient and pleasant way.

Revise, again and again

One of the best ways to improve and not get stuck at a basic level without evolving is to go back to what you have already learned and to revise. Forgetting is part of the process of learning and a totally natural phenomenon that happens to all students.

This is why revising, reviewing regularly what you have learned but that you may have forgotten, is so important. Don't worry if you make the same mistake over and over, the day when you've assimilated what you constantly forget, it will remain in your mind for good. It is only through revision and repetition that you can assimilate what you are learning.

Going back to what you have learned and forgotten will also help you memorize better and improve.

A quick reminder of the various ways to practice

—Read our free *French Accent Magazine*, listen to the audio links several times, have fun doing our crossword puzzle (with words taken from the magazine, which means that it will help a lot if you've read it beforehand!) and try to do the *dictées*.

—Keep the habit of **having regular lessons with your teacher** until you feel that you have reached a sufficient level and are able to improve your knowledge on your own.

—Use an **English-French dictionary** each time you have a doubt about the meaning of a word, there are many good ones online or as apps. We give a few suggestions of good ones in the Annex of this book.

—Use **all the free learning materials** that you can find on the web. We have included in the Annex the ones most frequently used by our students.

—Listen to everything in French **that pleases you**: songs, audio books, etc. and watch movies or TV series... You'll see a list of them in the Annex.

—Several times a week, every day if possible, **read an article in French or a post on a Facebook page or a blog...**

—Everyday if possible, read a few pages of **a book written in French**.

—Write in French as a homework assignment given by your teacher or to French people that you know or that you meet through social media. Let them correct you.

—In all cases, **make the maximum use of all the possibilities offered by YouTube and the social media**. Browse the web until you find a Facebook group, for example, in which it would be fun to participate. Making friends through the web is getting even easier after so many months of confinement!

Communicate with French-speaking people whenever possible

Traveling in France or in a French-speaking country is obviously an excellent way to practice. But you can also participate in French-speaking groups on Zoom or webinars when you cannot travel. So many possibilities of connecting with Francophones exist now on the web and social media.

Wherever you live, there is probably a French *Alliance Française* close by. They all organize events or encounters that you might like to attend. They also usually have a very good library and selection of French media.

Think about an immersion experience

Immerse yourself in France, in a French family or in a French-speaking environment, is another excellent way to practice intensely and to learn much more. It is even better when French native teachers organize an immersion workshop or take part in them by adding lessons to the program. You'll find on the web a good range of immersion courses organized by schools or private teachers all over France, and elsewhere. There are also good French immersions in non-French speaking countries. It may be a good idea to ask your teacher's advice before signing up.

The founders of Learn French at home, Céline Van Loan and Vincent Anthonioz, have organized many times in the past such immersions at their home and at the homes of other teachers. They always made it a fun and rewarding experience and were impressed by the results. Since 2019, Céline starting to organize once or twice a year a two-day immersion in Southern California close to her home in the form of a workshop. Three have already taken place, in Santa Barbara and in Ojai. All the participants said that it was one of the best opportunity to practice they have ever had!

Therefore, we really encourage you to think about an immersion experience in a workshop or a homestay in a French family. It is also a good way to immerse yourself a little in French culture.

TO REMEMBER FROM CHAPTER 13

Practice is an essential part of learning. *In this chapter,* we give you **a few tips on how to practice in an efficient way.**

• **Revise, again and again.**

• **Read our list of the various ways to practice.**

• **Communicate with French-speaking people** whenever possible.

• **Participate in an immersion.** There is no better way to practice if you can't live in a French-speaking country or with French people.

14. THE FUN PART: USING FRENCH EXPRESSIONS, AND REALIZING HOW BEING FLUENT HAS CHANGED YOU

AN ASPECT OF THE FRENCH language that all our students love is the multitude of idiomatic expressions constantly used by the French in daily conversations ! They are widespread in English, too, but they're almost always different in French and it's always entertaining to compare these expressions between the two languages.

Some of them are very funny! A few examples among thousands:

—*Il pleut comme vache qui pisse* (lit.: It rains like a cow that pisses), or *Il pleut des cordes* (lit.: it rains ropes) = It rains cats and dogs.

—*Filer à l'anglaise* (lit: to flee the English way) = to take French leave.

—*Se payer la tête de quelqu'un* (lit.: to buy for oneself someone's head) = to pull somebody's leg.

—*Avoir d'autres chats à fouetter* (lit.: to have other cats to whip) = to have other fish to fry.

—*Cracher dans la soupe* (lit.: to spit in the soup) = to bite the hand that feeds you.

—*Casser sa pipe* (lit.: to break one's pipe) = to kick the bucket.

—*Coûter la peau des fesses* (lit.: to cost the skin of the butt) = to cost an arm and a leg.

—*C'est la cerise sur le gâteau* (lit.: It's the cherry on the cake) = It's the icing on the cake.

The day you start being able to use one of them in the best appropriate manner it's really the icing on the cake! And mainly because it is important. If you hope to be able to speak like a real French person some day, you have to know the most popular ones. First, they're extremely useful if you want to understand a conversation between French people as they use so many of them without even thinking of it. And later, you'll consider it almost as a major step and even a little victory when you are able to use one yourself in a conversation. Our students feel so proud the day that happens to them!

Teaching the more currently used ones is part of the lessons or the homework we give. It's quite often the occasion for a good laugh.

We also encourage our readers of our magazine *French Accent* to discover a few more in the regular column *"Le coin des branchés"* illustrated with a little drawing to make them easier to understand and memorize. Reading articles, watching movies and listening to songs are other ways to familiarize yourself with new expressions.

Where do they come from? That is the question

As soon as they learn and memorize an expression that they know, the students almost always inevitably come to us and tell us: "Such a bizarre expression"! We can only agree, sometimes realizing for the first time how strange it is. And then they ask us: "Why? Where does it come from"? Of course, like most French people, we have no idea and we have to search on Google or in our dictionaries. Having an etymological dictionary at hand is very useful in this respect... The majority of such expressions come from very old traditions, myths or legends that have been totally forgotten, and it happens that there are often various versions of the supposed origin.

From time to time, it's our students themselves who tell us the origin of the expression that they found before we did.

My own husband Roger, who is an American teacher of French language and literature, knows many of them and their origin because, of course, he has the curiosity of a foreigner to look for the meaning. Recently he asked me: "Do you know the origin of *Revenons à nos moutons*"? (which means: Let's get back to the topic in hand; lit.: Let's go back to our sheep). As usual I had no clue. He was quite satisfied to explain to me that it comes from a theatre play, *La farce de maître Pathelin*, written by an unknown French author in the 15th century. He told me the full story: In a case of stolen sheep, Pathelin, in arguing his case before a judge, embarks on telling all kinds of stories about totally unrelated issues. The judge interrupts him with: *Revenons à nos moutons !*

Digging further your knowledge of French will help you re-discover your own language

As we always say, a captivating aspect of teaching French (or any another language) is that we learn a lot about everything that our students tell us about their life, they work, their activity, the knowledge they share, the culture of their countries, etc. But we learn, or re-discover also, a great deal about our own language and even about our own culture.

It is the same for our students, as they all tell us when they've reached an advanced level. By learning French, they have a natural tendency to analyze more their mother tongue, to observe, to learn even some aspects of the grammar and to pay more attention to the vocabulary. Also, they look at their own idiomatic expressions with external eyes and appreciate more their awkwardness.

When you notice that becoming fluent in French has changed you

There is no doubt that when you become fluent, you will discover that there is now something French in you. But there is even more: Being fluent in another language makes you a distinctly different person. This is what most of the students who have reached a very good level tell us.

It is well known that many people change their attitude depending on which language they express themselves in. The tone of the voice changes and even the body language. But it goes even beyond: Their way of looking at other people has evolved. Several students told us that by learning French they've become more tolerant towards people from other cultures, they're interested in finding out even more about them.

We always say that learning a language is learning its culture, which is something we all experienced when we studied English. There is a stage when the appeal of learning French has become the appeal of gaining a deeper understanding of the French people, with all their contradictions and their complexity. You also wish to know more about a culture that has insidiously made a mark on you. Immersing yourself into French has changed you into a different person. You'll probably never become totally French but you'll have the immense pleasure of having enriched your own personal culture.

TO REMEMBER FROM CHAPTER 14

- **Enjoy discovering many very funny French idiomatic expressions!**

- **These expressions are extremely useful** if you want to understand **a conversation between French people.**

- **You'll be so proud the day you are able to use some of them** in a conversation!

- **Challenge your teacher** by finding out **where they come from.**

- Notice how by deepening your knowledge of French **you will re-discover your own language.**

- And one day, you will realize that **becoming fluent has changed you.**

Jim, our model student

"ONE OF MY FAVORITE things to do in Paris is nothing. By nothing, I mean just wandering around with only a vague plan of where to go and stumble upon something great. Breakfast, walking around the city, lunch in another café or a picnic in a park, more walking, maybe a museum hit, *apéro*-time, dinner in a great bistro, walking after dinner, metro home — this is a good day."

"Meeting people, chatting with them,
is the best part of visiting a country"

Jim Merical, a computer technician specialist, is our model student. In our previous self-help book published in 2016, *Learn French? Of Course You Can!*, where he appears on the cover, we quoted him all along as he is such an inspiration for all French learners. Jim has been amazing. When he started learning French with us in 2005, he had no knowledge of the language whatsoever. He lives in California and rarely has the chance to go to France. Still, since the beginning his motivation has been remarkable.

He was one of Céline's first students. Over the years, he never stopped taking French lessons with Learn French at Home. But, far from limiting himself to taking lessons, he always went the extra mile to learn French and created a wide range of ways to constantly practice in order to improve his French in spite of his very busy professional schedule. We find his experience so inspiring for all students that we couldn't end this book without sharing it with all those who, like him, dream of becoming fluent.

Jim loves everything in France. "I also adore the French language. It has always held an allure for me, but I don't really understand why. I was 15 when I first decided to learn French. But I really started at the age of 45, and could only learn from a distance, by Skype.

Since my first lesson with Céline some fifteen years ago, learning French was terrific! I just loved it. I have never stopped taking them.

"Over the years my motivation has been the driving force of all the efforts I have made over the years and that I continue to make: I want to be able to communicate with the French during each of my trips to France. For me, meeting people, chatting with them, listening to them, is the best part of visiting a country."

Jim spends a lot of time driving, going from one client to the other. For him, this is the best time to listen to the French podcasts he has previously downloaded: French radio programs or recorded French lessons. He alternates with French songs or French news. In the evening before going to bed he reads a few pages of a French novel in the original language. His discipline, apart from his lessons, includes a few other activities several times a week. On weekends, when he has more time, Jim loves watching French movies and, when subtitles are available, he prefers the subtitles in French. He also enjoys spending time over an aperitif or a dinner with French friends. And even when he is gardening on Saturday morning he listens to French podcasts on his iPhone.

Over time, Jim and his wife Leslie have become very good friends of all of us. We all enjoy watching French movies together or spending time over a dinner, speaking French only and laughing while commenting on the French news but also on articles and cartoons from the *Canard enchaîné**.

"Reading a book in French is a very slow adventure, like a day of sailing"

Jim also loves reading books written in French, mainly novels, but also an essay from time to time. "I read slowly because I needed to look up so many words in my dictionary," he explains. "I find the *Ultralingua* dictionary on my iPhone very effective and useful. My first 'real' book in French was *Le Petit Prince*, by Antoine de Saint-Exupéry, which I have read again and again and that is still one of my favorite books, even if I hate the fact that so many verbs are conjugated in the *passé simple*.

"When I read a book which is particularly difficult, with an advanced vocabulary and grammar, finding the meaning of many phrases or paragraphs is a very slow adventure. It is like a day of sailing — it is very pleasant, but we make very slow progress".

Jim wants to give another piece of advice for French learn-

© Céline Van Loan

ers: "Over time, I have learned that when I have a conversation with French people, I need to give up the idea of understanding absolutely everything. It's much more interesting, less stressful and much easier to follow the flow of the conversation if I'm not blocked by one word or another." And regarding expressing himself in French, he adds, jokingly: "It's OK if we lose 3/4 of our intelligence (at least in the eyes of others) when we try to have a conversation in their language, compared to when we express ourselves in our own language"!

He further explains that "learning French is definitely not a straight line. It seems that I spend long periods without making any progress and then, suddenly, my level has improved. Now, I love to travel not only to Paris but to any little village in any region of France, anywhere I won't risk meeting people who speak English"! And he does so. When we travel together in France, he feels such a real joy and satisfaction speaking in French that he's always the first to speak to everybody we meet!

---

* A weekly satirical French newspaper.

15. CHILDREN LOVE
LEARNING FRENCH, TOO!

WITH THE COVID-19 CONFINEMENT, the demand for lessons for children increased more than ever before. Parents were forced to act as associate teachers to help their kids who were taking their classes on Zoom. And they realized the need to complement such classes with private distance lessons (also through Skype or Zoom) with other teachers. This would also have the advantage of keeping their children a little more busy while they had to work themselves from home! And then came the vacation: another good time to get the kids to take language lessons and do something both fun and intelligent that could prove very useful in their adult life.

It is a very well known fact that children are like sponges with languages, learning so fast that this can be challenging for their parents who cannot always keep up with them.

Children can also quickly acquire the right accent. Studies have shown that learning one or several languages is excellent for their development and definitely positive for their future whatever they choose to do when they get older. Therefore, we can only encourage parents to give their children the opportunity to learn a second language, and not just in school.

To be bilingual: a wonderful asset for the future

There are a multitude of advantages in being bilingual, and it is even more so the case for children in a globalized world when you can communicate instantaneously with people from any part of the planet. Most parents are very much aware that their kids will benefit from knowing more than one language and language education is encouraged, starting in preschools. Exposing your child to a second language will help them learn about other cultures. Bilinguals tend to be more creative thinkers than those who speak only one language, and their brain functions can even stay sharper as they age.

Equally important, learning a second language doesn't interfere with learning their native language properly. Many reports have specifically demonstrated that children who have learned a second language earn higher SAT scores, particularly on the verbal section of the test. And people who are being interviewed for a job and who possess more than one language will find it much easier, whatever profession they might choose, to be selected from among candidates who master only their native language. This may have a major impact on their career and on their whole life.

At what age to start?

We are constantly asked this question. Actually, there is no definite rule, no specific age and it is never too late to start. Many specialists would say that the earlier the better. For children who start very early, between 2 to 3 years old, the second language may immediately become a second nature as they absorb so quickly whatever they hear. They can learn to understand new words in two different languages at an incredibly fast rate. Therefore, the earlier you introduce a second language, the easier it will be for your child to pick it up and to have native-like pronunciation.

But even if they start a little later, for example between 6 to 12, they can still, depending on the situation, the reasons for choosing a language and the motivation, absorb a new language extremely quickly and even become totally bilingual. And if they start learning before the onset of adolescence, they are as likely to acquire native-like pronunciation as younger children.

What method to choose?

The choice of the teaching method is very important. Not so many schools offer French lessons for kids, and except for some very exclusive and expensive private schools the teaching might not be so good. In public schools in the US, most teachers aren't French natives and even if they are good, extremely motivated and devoted instructors for whom we have the deepest respect, many struggle with the pronunciation and, sadly, make mistakes.

If your children have the chance to be offered extracurricular programs taking place on weekends or after school, this may help them to improve a lot. However, making the children work overtime to learn a language is not always very well received and does not prove very productive, unless they are extremely motivated. It is also time consuming for the parents. Not very many schools offer excellent opportunities for learning other languages anyway, and such programs are not always easily accessible.

Learning by Skype or Zoom? The kids love it — and it works!

This is why taking lessons from home, at a convenient time from the kid, through Skype or Zoom is so appropriate! We realized this need long ago. As early as 2007, we created a special program of "French lessons for kids" that was designed for children from 6 to 12. Quickly we could confirm what we were convinced of: that kids learn very fast and are generally attracted and motivated to learn if the lesson is performed in a relaxed and fun atmosphere. Equally rapidly, we could witness how they found taking their lesson via Skype and Zoom exciting, mainly because kids love to use the computer and appreciate the real time interaction!

The lessons last only 30 to 45 minutes but with a pair of earphones, a webcam and some visual teaching material, the kids do not see the time pass. The teacher targets the lesson's objective towards comprehension through games, pictures, drawings, small role plays, songs and more. All of them are fundamental to keep the student's attention during the entire lesson.

And there is some homework to do! The lessons can be taken on a weekday or on a weekend at any suitable time for the child, who feels very comfortable taking them in their room, surrounded by their own books, toys, dolls or stuffed animals, which often participate in the lesson...

Sometimes, it happens that the mother or the father joins the child during the lesson, offering their help or because they are simply curious to see how it goes. However, several parents told us that their child makes them understand immediately that they aren't welcome. They say: "Mom, please, we are working!" And then, when it is time for the next lesson, the child goes to their room and before closing the door, tells the parents: "See you later! Now it's time for my lesson with MY French teacher."

Andrea Renaud, the mother of two kids who started classes with Learn French at Home in 2015, told us in 2020, after five years of weekly lessons for both of them: "The lessons have been wonderful for my children. Both Drew and Megan really enjoyed learning from you and continuing their French education."

Since its creation, the children's lessons on Skype have been one of our most successful programs. Apart from teaching a second language to children who have no access to foreign language lessons at school or close to their home, it is also very much used by parents who are homeschooling by choice or by necessity, as it was the case when under lockdown. During the confinement, many children who were being homeschooled were studying French through our program.

One-on-one lessons are reassuring

Since the confinement, not only such long distance lessons were efficient in helping both the parents and the kids, but also the children loved them because they found it reassuring to have such an "intimate" contact with a teacher in a one-on-one lesson on Skype or Zoom. Even if they had fun watching their school teachers and their friends on a group Zoom screen, they felt some stress and couldn't be as relaxed as they were in a school room where they could discreetly chat with friends or laugh with them. Many parents told us that, for their kids, having only for themselves a teacher who is very positive, encouraging and who makes them have fun while learning through games, was a reassuring element. They felt more comfortable and more confident.

And when they aren't children anymore, they still go on!

Many kids who have been our students for a long time find these lessons so great and fun, and they love them so much, that they don't want to stop them, even when they aren't children anymore! We have many young students who were 8 or 10 when they started in 2012-2013. They are now 15 to 17 and they still have their usual lessons, often with the same teacher.

TO REMEMBER FROM CHAPTER 15

- **During the confinement, the demand for French lessons for kids increased considerably.**

- **Children absorb foreign languages like sponges,** learning so fast that **this can be challenging for their parents** who cannot always keep up with them!

- **To be bilingual will be a wonderful asset for their future.**

- **At what age to start?** There is **no definite rule, no specific age** and **it is never too late to start.**

- **The choice of the best method is very important,** but not always easy.

- **Children love taking lessons by Skype or Zoom** with a French native teacher as we do at Learn French at home since 2009, and **it works! They make wonderful progress** through this way of teaching.

- **Taking one-on-one lessons with a teacher they know very well, who cares and is very nice, is a reassuring element,** especially compare to group Zoom classes.

- **And when they're not children anymore, many still want to continue!**

SHAMBHALA PUBLICATIONS

If you'd like to receive a copy of our latest catalogue of books and audios, please fill out and return this card. It's easy—the postage is already paid!

Or, if you'd prefer, you can e-mail us at CustomerCare@shambhala.com, sign up online at www.shambhala.com/newsletter, or call toll-free (888) 424-2329.

NAME

ADDRESS

CITY / STATE / ZIP / COUNTRY

E-MAIL

And by also giving us your e-mail address, you'll automatically be signed up to receive news about new releases, author events, and special offers!

ANNEX: OUR SUGGESTIONS OF USEFUL RESOURCES

1. Online dictionaries and applications

—Word Reference
Free and multilingual, and a good app on any device.
www.wordreference.com

—Linguee
Excellent, online or as an app, as it not only gives the translation but also examples of contexts in which the words and expressions are used:
https://www.linguee.com

—DeepL
Launched by Linguee, DeepL is for now the best online translator. Even if there are always a few mistakes. You can use it freely on your computer or smartphone (no app, though) or subscribe to the version PRO, with fees adapted to your needs.
https://www.deepl.com/translator

—Collins
A good free dictionary and app:
www.collinsdictionary.com/dictionary/english-french

2. General learning and grammar websites and apps

Duolingo
A free learning program that is very popular among all students: www.duolingo.com

Other sites:
www.tolearnfrench.com
http://french.about.com
www.reverso.net/text_translation.aspx?lang=FR
www.bonjourdefrance.com/index/indexgram.htm
https://apps.carleton.edu/curricular/fren/Language_tools

3. Tools for French verb conjugation

www.verbix.com
https://la-conjugaison.nouvelobs.com
http://leconjugueur.lefigaro.fr/php5/index.php?verbe
www.laits.utexas.edu/tex/gr/tap10.html

4. Vocabulary and idiomatic expressions

www.expressio.fr
www.languageguide.org/french/
http://lexiquefle.free.fr
www.digitaldialects.com/French.htm
http://doyouspeaktouriste.fr/#&panel1-1

5. Free French podcasts

www.podcastfrancaisfacile.com
www.french-podcasts.com
https://direct-radio.fr/recherche/podcast

6. Radio stations live & replay

France Info:
www.francetvinfo.fr

RFI:
www.rfi.fr/en/france
Europe 1:
https://www.europe1.fr
France Culture:
www.franceculture.fr

7. Television stations live & replay

—**TV5Monde:**
http://parlons-francais.tv5monde.com/webdocumentaires-pour-apprendre-le-francais/p-1-lg0-Accueil.htm
—**TV7:**
www.tv7.com
—**Radio Télévision suisse (RTS):**
www.rts.ch

8. Song lyrics

Here is a selection of websites that present many song lyrics in French (you'll find all the songs on YouTube, Spotify, etc.):
—**Wiki Paroles** (less ads on this one):
http://fr.lyrics.wikia.com/wiki/WikiaParoles
—**ParolesMania:**
www.parolesmania.com
—**Paroles.net:**
www.paroles.net

9. Articles from the media to read online

—French Accent magazine

Our publication is an essential **e-magazine** (pdf format) for French learners. It has a central theme, articles on politics, culture, grammar, cinema and literature. With scenarios, glossaries dictations and audio links that will definitely help you improve your French. *French Accent* appears every two months, and **the subscription is free**:
www.learnfrenchathome.com/french-accent-magazine

—Le Monde

This French daily newspaper that we consider the best makes more news articles accessible to non-subscribers than its competitors.
www.lemonde.fr

—Courrier International

French learning students like this very well-done weekly magazine. It is indeed easier to understand as all the articles are translations from publications in another language. But you have to subscribe to have full access to the articles. The cost is about US$ 6 a month for the digital version (online or app).
www.courrierinternational.com

10. Films available on Netflix, Amazon or streaming

Here is a short selection. We added the title in English of the French versions (not of remakes, that we never recommend):

—*Trois hommes et un couffin* (Title in English: *Three Men and a Craddle*), 1985.
—*Tanguy* (same title in English), 2001.
—*L'Auberge espagnole* (3 different titles for the French versions: *Pot Luck* in the UK, *L'Auberge espagnole* in the US and *The Spanish Apart-*

ment in Australia) 2002. It was such a such success that two sequels were made later on with the same actors, both very good:
Les Poupées russes (*Russian Dolls*), 2005, and **Le Casse-tête chinois** (*Chinese Puzzle*), 2013.
—**Prête-moi ta main** (*I Do*), 2006.
—**Intouchables** (*The Intouchables*), 2011.
—**Le Prénom** (*What's in a Name?*), 2012.
—**Les saveurs du Palais** (*Haute Cuisine*), 2012.
—**Tokyo Fiancée** (same title in English), 2015.
—**Sage-femme** (*The Midwife*), 2017.
—**Mademoiselle de Joncquière** (*Lady J.*), 2018.
—**Deux moi** (*Someone, Somewhere*), 2018.
—**Chambre 212** (*On a Magical Night*), 2019.
—**Le mystère Henri Pick** (*The Mystery of Henri Pick*), 2019.

11. TV Séries (in French: *Séries télé*) **available on Netflix, Amazon or streaming**

—**Un village français** (Title in English: *A French village*); 7 seasons, a total of 72 episodes. Since 2009.
—**Dix pour cent** (*Call my agent*); 4 seasons of 6 episodes. Since 2015.
—**Marseille** (same title en anglais); 2 seasons of 8 episodes. Since 2016.
—**Le Bazar de la Charité** (*The Bonfire of Destiny*): 1 season of 8 episodes, 2019.

12. Books

Our fiction Short Stories in French with audio:
12 Short suspense Stories in French for French Learners
—**Le bruit des vagues. Nr. 1, 2017.**
—**Le pays de l'amour. Nr. 2, 2018.**
—**Le trésor. Nr 3, 2019.**
—**Le chat qui parle. Nr 4, 2020.**

All these short suspense stories with a little surprise at the end are accompanied with glossaries, grammar, vocabulary tips and cultural notes explained in English and exercises (solutions at the end). They all have audio links from which you can listen to the whole story in French. You can choose between the eBook version (pdf) that you can purchase on our website or the paperback, available on Amazon. Inside the paperback version, a link gives you access to the eBook version and to the audio.

To purchase the eBook (pdf) version:
www.learnfrenchathome.com/french-audio-books
To purchase the paperback version:
amazon.com/author/annickstevenson

A few classics:
—*La gloire de mon père* and *Le château de ma mère,* by Marcel Pagnol.
—*Le petit Nicolas.* Series of short stories about the adventures of a young boy, Nicolas, by Jean-Jacques Sempé, beautifully illustrated by Goscinny.

Some good novels:
—*L'élégance du hérisson,* by Muriel Barbery. This amazing novel was adapted into a movie: *Le hérisson* (in English: *The Hedgehog*).
—*Le tour du monde du roi Zibeline,* by Jean-Christophe Rufin. Most of his books are captivating.
—*Sentinelle de la pluie,* by Tatiana de Rosnay. All her other books are excellent, too.
—*Changer l'eau des fleurs,* by Valérie Perrin, a wonderful novel. Her first one, *Les oubliés du dimanche,* was also really great.
—*La vie d'une autre,* by Frédérique Deghelt. This excellent novel, which was her first one, has been adapted into a movie (title in English: *Another Woman's Life*). She published many others since then, all different and interesting to read.

A few other authors:
Among the contemporary novelists that our students find not too difficult to read are also:
—**Marc Lévy**, who publishes a book every year, always a bestseller.
—**Guillaume Musso**, who is also among the authors who sells the most books in France. He publishes a new novel almost every year.
—**Amélie Nothomb**, a Belgian novelist living in Paris. All her novels are bestsellers and they have also the advantage of being very short.
—**Aki Shimazaki**, a Japanese author who lives in Canada and writes in French. . For example, her series of five short novels, *Le Poids des secrets*, is very easy to read and is both moving and captivating.
—**Akira Mizubayashi**, a Japanese professor and author who loves so much the French language that he writes in French all his essays and novels (see one of his quotes on page 7). We can recommend his essay *Une langue venue d'ailleurs*, an excellent motivation book for students. *Un amour de Mille-Ans* is one of his very good novels.

13. Learning tools for children

There is a multitude of websites of teaching material for children. The ones we recommend below make the children learn through games and songs.

Games and exercises:
www.ortholud.com
www.jeuxdememoire.net
www.education.vic.gov.au/LanguagesOnline/french/french.htm

Children's songs:
http://comptines.tv
www.mondedestitounis.fr/chanson-enfant.php

How to access the eBook version

With the purchase of this paperback, you have access to the eBook version, in pdf format.

One advantage is that while consulting it you can enlarge the text (to 125%, 150% or more). Also, if you read it from a computer, when searching for a word it's very easy to find it by typing "Control F" on your keyboard.

Here is the link for a free copy of the eBook version:
www.learnfrenchathome.com/magazine/learnfrench/
LearningFrench_eb.pdf

About the author

Annick Stevenson is a French journalist, writer and translator. For some 25 years, she was an international journalist and magazine editor for the United Nations.

She has published and translated several books and she is the author or co-author of all the books published by Learn French at Home. She is also the editor of our free *French Accent magazine*.

www.learnfrenchathome.com/french-accent-magazine
amazon.com/author/annickstevenson

LEARN FRENCH ──── AT HOME

Learn French at Home, created in 2004 by Céline and Vincent Anthonioz, has helped thousands of French learners, each with very different learning goals. The main ingredient of our success lies in our team of professional and friendly native French teachers who take the time to personalize every single lesson according to the student's personal and professional goal. Our main purpose is to deliver true quality service to each student. It doesn't matter where you live as the lessons take place in the student's home or workplace. The teachers are located in several countries.

When you're ready to take your French learning to another level, *Learn French at Home* can set you up with one-on-one personalized French lessons with a professional and encouraging French native teacher. Every lesson is given on Skype or Zoom. Whether you need to learn the language to prepare for your upcoming trip to a French speaking country, or whether you need it to work on any professional objectives, or you simply wish to enjoy communicating in French, you'll find the appropriate program on our website. We also offer French lessons for kids, which are a big success among parents. During the session on Skype or Zoom, the teacher privileges that time to stimulate the learner to speak in French, and explains grammatical points. You'll get real practice as though you were traveling or living in France!

We offer 9 different lesson formats, you can read about them on:

www.learnfrenchathome.com

To find out if learning French on Skype or Zoom is right for you, schedule a **free one-on-one evaluation**:

www.learnfrenchathome.com/free-french-lessons

Bienvenue à Learn French at Home !

Every teacher at Learn French at Home teaches French with passion and establishes a caring and friendly relationship with each student. Learning from home in a relaxed atmosphere inevitably leads to positive results. Having fun learning while experiencing real progress is our main objective for each lesson.

À bientôt !

Céline

Made in the USA
Middletown, DE
19 January 2021